Depression in Children
and Adolescents

Depression in Children and Adolescents

Edited by
Kedar Nath Dwivedi
and
Ved Prakash Varma

SINGULAR PUBLISHING GROUP, INC.
SAN DIEGO, CALIFORNIA

© 1997 Whurr Publishers Ltd

First Published 1997 by
Whurr Publishers Ltd
19b Compton Terrace, London N1 2UN, England

Published and Distributed in the
United States and Canada by
SINGULAR PUBLISHING GROUP, INC.
401 West A Street, Suite 325
San Diego, CA 92101, USA

British Library Cataloguing in Publication Data
A catalogue record for this book is available from the
British Library.

ISBN 1-897635-92-3

Singular Number 1-56593-835-6

Printed and bound in the UK by Athenaeum Press Ltd,
Gateshead, Tyne & Wear

Contents

Dedication

The editors dedicate this book, with warm affection and esteem, to Dr O.N. Srivastava, formerly Professor and Head of the Department of Psychiatry, Institute of Medical Sciences, Banaras Hindu University, Varanasi, India, and subsequently Director, Residency Training Programme, Rosenburg Psychiatric Centre, The Hague, Netherlands.

Professor Srivastava: an Appreciation

It was a great pleasure and privilege to be invited to write an appreciation of Professor O.N. Srivastava, a legendary teacher and clinician for more than three decades. Professor Srivastava became involved with psychiatry at a time when the discipline in India was beginning to move beyond the mental hospitals and was struggling to find its rightful place as an academic field within medical faculties. The depth and expanse of his knowledge, his dedication to his subject, his excellence as a clinician and his organizational astuteness worked wonders during this critical period and earned psychiatry a respectable place in medicine both at the Medical Institute in Varanasi and throughout India. His deep, penetrating and analytical insight into clinical problems, his multifaceted understanding of clinical phenomena, and his refreshing humaneness inspired successive generations of students and trainee psychiatrists both in India and in the Netherlands where he trained successive generations of psychiatrists. His charisma as a teacher, clinician and researcher drew the best medical graduates to psychiatry and helped it to become one of the most coveted specializations in Varanasi. In India, and later in the Netherlands, he was always a popular and highly esteemed teacher and he was the role model *par excellence* for his trainees. He had the rare ability to inculcate a spirit of enquiry in his students.

In his approach to psychiatry, Professor Srivastava always rejected a narrow sectarian view and emphasized the biopsycho-social approach in full. He looked upon psychiatry not as a field exclusively for specialists but rather as a basic science for all physicians, irrespective of their specializations. It was this approach that led him to persuade the medical faculty in Varanasi to allocate time in the medical curriculum for the teaching of psychiatry from the very first year of medical studies.

His research interests were wide and touched upon the biological as well as the psycho-social dimensions of psychiatry, but psychiatric epidemiology always held a special fascination for him as an area of research. His wide erudition, even outside his field of specialization, and his openness to cultural influences, helped him to appreciate the important role that cultural factors play in the causation, presentation and perpetuation of psychiatric disorders. At the same time he never lost sight of the manner in which the family influences the shaping of the personality and the presentation and prognosis of disease. It was only natural that these cultural and family factors were emphasized both in his teaching and in his clinical practice.

His appreciation of the crucial role that the family plays in psychiatric disorders, particularly in Indian culture with its extended family structures, led him to involve families extensively when treating individuals. At the University Psychiatric Clinic in Varanasi, which Professor Srivastava established and headed, it was standard practice to allow patients' families to stay with them day and night.

It is only fitting that Dr Dwivedi and Dr Varma, editors of this book, have dedicated it to such an esteemed teacher and clinician. The book is a particularly appropriate tribute to the teachings and philosophy of Professor Srivastava as it takes a multifaceted and wide-ranging view of depression in children and adolescents. It approaches the phenomenology and etiology of depression employing a broad framework and covers the various approaches to treatment from all angles (various forms of psychotherapy find a place side-by-side with pharmacological approaches, for example). One of the editors of this book (Dr Dwivedi), like the writer of this appreciation, was a student of Professor Srivastava and the fact that Professor Srivastava's eclectic approach to clinical problems has been reflected in *Depression in Children and Adolescents* is a testimony to the strength of his teaching and philosophy

Prakash B. Behere, MBBS, MD, MNAMS,
Professor of Psychiatry, Mahatma Gandhi Institute of Medical Sciences, Sevagram, Wardha and formerly Reader in Psychiatry at Varanasi.

About the Contributors

Dr Philip Barker is Professor in the Departments of Psychiatry and Paediatrics at the University of Calgary, Canada, and Director of the Department of Psychiatry at the Alberta Children's Hospital, Calgary. He is the author of seven books and the co-author of one. His *Basic Child Psychiatry*, first published in 1971 and now in its sixth edition, has become a standard introductory text on child psychiatry. Professor Barker is the author of many papers in scientific journals, and has contributed numerous chapters to books relating to his field.

Muriel Barrett worked in primary schools in London, and then at the Tavistock Centre with children of all age groups, and their families. She was also the organizing tutor for a postgraduate training course for teachers. She has undertaken workshops and teaching in Britain and overseas and, after her retirement, inaugurated the International Educational Therapy conferences.

Dr Julian Brockless is Consultant in Child and Adolescent Psychiatry in the East Berkshire Community Health National Health Service Trust. He served as Chair of the Local Child Protection Review Committee (1990–1992), as the lead clinician for the Trust's Child and Adolescent Psychiatry Services (1992–1996), and as the Chair of the East Berkshire Division of Psychiatry from 1992.

Dr Finn Cosgrove has been a consultant since 1979. He works in Bristol and has a particular interest in attention deficit hyperactivity disorder. He is one of only two child psychiatrist members of the British Association of Psychopharmacology, and specializes in the use of psychotropic medication with children and adolescents.

Dr Ingrid Davison is Consultant in Child and Family Psychiatry with the Leicestershire Child and Family Psychiatric Service. She has wide experience in the assessment and treatment of children and their families and has a particular interest in group interventions with children and parents and in the training of fellow professionals.

Dr Kedar Nath Dwivedi is Consultant in Child, Adolescent and Family Psychiatry at the Child and Family Consultation Service and the Ken Stewart Family Centre, Northampton. He is also clinical teacher in the Faculty of Medicine, University of Leicester. Dr Dwivedi graduated in medicine from the Institute of Medical Sciences, Varanasi, India, and served as Assistant Professor in Preventive and Social Medicine in Simla before coming to Britain in 1974. Since then he has worked in psychiatry and is a member of more than a dozen professional associations. Dr Dwivedi has contributed to nearly forty publications. This includes editing the well-received *Groupwork with Children and Adolescents* (1993), *Therapeutic Use of Stories* (in press), and *Enhancing Parenting Skills* (in press). He also co-edited *Meeting the Needs of Ethnic Minority Children (1996)* and *Management of Childhood Anxiety Disorders* (in press). He is interested in eastern approaches to mental health, especially those of Buddhism.

Dr Mary Evans is Senior Registrar in Child and Adolescent Psychiatry in Sheffield. She has used cognitive therapy techniques in individual work with children, adolescents and adults. Together with Ann Murphy she has developed a cognitive-behavioural therapy group for children who have reached the stage of latency.

Joan Hutten worked as Principal Social Worker in the Child and Family Department of the Tavistock Clinic, London, where she initiated a multi-disciplinary programme for brief focal intervention and was responsible for training. She now has a consultancy practice catering for individuals, groups and institutions.

Dr Graham Curtis Jenkins worked as a general practitioner pediatrician in a large group practice outside London for 28 years. He developed an experimental, comprehensive child care programme for children under three years of age, incorporating a child and family consultation service, and has written extensively on the subject. He resigned from the National Health Service in 1991 to become the first Director of the Counselling in Primary Care Trust formed to promote, support and develop counselling, psychotherapy and the use of counselling skills in general practice. He has also trained as a psychotherapist.

Ann Murphy has worked in child and adolescent mental health teams for 11 years and is a community psychiatric nurse in Sheffield. She has wide experience of group work and, together with Mary Evans, has developed a cognitive-behavioural therapy group for children who have reached the latency stage.

Judith Waterfield taught in mainstream primary schools before conducting multidisciplinary work in a hospital setting with individual children, adolescent groups, families and schools. She was a tutor for a training course in educational therapy techniques and is currently an adviser for special learning needs at Plymouth University, England.

Dr Ved Prakash Varma was formerly an educational psychologist with the Institute of Education, University of London, the Tavistock Clinic, and the London Borough of Richmond and Brent. He has edited and co-edited more than 30 books on education, psychology, psychiatry, psychotherapy and social work and has been an international figure in the field of special needs.

Biddy Youell works as a Child and Adolescent Psychotherapist in Buckinghamshire and north London. Before undertaking the Child Psychotherapy training at the Tavistock Clinic, she was a teacher and worked in a variety of mainstream schools and special educational settings in inner London. She has a particular interest in the effect of emotional difficulties on children's ability to learn and in the ways which psychoanalytic understanding can inform practice in educational institutions.

Preface

There has been a growing awareness of the need to take the problem of childhood depression more seriously. It is sometimes felt that there is a lack of high quality practical material to help professionals assist children and adolescents with depression today. Both Ved Varma and myself have been acutely aware of the need for such material for some time and we feel that this book will go a long way to meet it.

I am very grateful to Ved for his active encouragement in instigating this project and for the extensive editorial experience that he brought with him. It has been an immense pleasure to help create this important book, particularly because all the contributions have been of such a high standard. Moreover, the experience of working with such a diverse multidisciplinary team of experts has been challenging, exciting and educationally rewarding. The team included specialists in child, adolescent and family psychiatry, child psychotherapy, social work, community psychiatric nursing, educational therapy, the coordination of special needs in teaching, and general practice.

We are deeply indebted to all the contributors, some of whom had to put up with our 'gentle' reminders about deadlines or requests for revisions. We are equally grateful to the publishers for their enthusiastic, sensitive, creative and painstakingly thorough approach to this very important project.

My special thanks to Carol Weller and Nicola Buckby from our library and to Dorothy Stephen, the librarian, as they have been most helpful in coping with so many of my 'a.s.a.p.' requests. I am also very grateful to my colleagues at the Child and Family Consultation Centre and the Ken Stewart Family Centre for their valuable support. I am particularly thankful to Karen Amos and to Naina Sadrani, my secretary, who has been the dynamic centre of our service. The birth of this book coincided with the birth of her daughter, Ria.

The support of my family – Radha, Amitabh, Amrita and Rajaneesh – has also been essential for me in this project.

Finally we would like to thank the reader for taking the trouble to read our book.

Kedar Nath Dwivedi

Introduction

KEDAR NATH DWIVEDI

There is now a growing recognition that children and adolescents have depressive disorders with features similar to those observed in adults. Research activity in this field has increased with this awareness and a great deal has recently appeared in the literature about childhood depression, including epidemiological aspects, pathogenesis, characteristics, assessment, links with other childhood and adult disorders, and treatment strategies. In fact, the diagnostic criteria in current ICD-10 and DSM-IV classifications are also broadly applicable to young people, particularly adolescents. In the past, child psychiatrists had mainly relied on parental reports for the diagnosis of depression in children, thinking that the parents knew everything about their children. It is now increasingly clear that children themselves can provide valuable information about their own psychopathology (Weller and Weller, 1990).

Depressive disorders in young people have been found to be more common than previously supposed (Goodyer, 1995). Depression has also become a major concern for schools because of its impact on learning and because of the risk of suicide. Schools now recognize it as a serious problem, responsible for lowering the social and academic functioning of children. It can be associated with negative peer evaluation, poor self-esteem, poor academic performance, hopelessness about lessons and tests, negative teacher evaluation, conduct disorder, social withdrawal, tearfulness, school refusal, poor concentration, distractibility and learning difficulties in the school context.

Many children suffering from depression may not appear overtly depressed, so there could be a problem of underidentification as depression can be easily overlooked if children do not actively seek attention.

Miezitis (1992), from Ontario, suggests that 5 to 10% of the normal school population have depression (prevalence is higher in adolescents,

and more so in girls); in fact a quarter of children considered by teachers to be distractible actually have features of depression, and 25% to
50% of learning disabled children have the condition. In prepubertal
children there appear to be no gender differences in prevalence rates of
depression; girls, however, seem to develop more risk factors for
depression than boys and face more new challenges than boys in early
adolescence. These factors may combine to generate gender differences
in depression beginning in early adolescence (Nolen-Hoeksema and
Girgus, 1994). In adolescent girls, Monck *et al.* (1994) found a 16.9%
prevalence of depression and anxiety disorders.

Angold and Costello (1993) highlight the degree of comorbidity with
depressive disorders in children. They found that the comorbidity with
conduct disorder and oppositional defiant disorder ranged from 21% to
83%, with anxiety disorders from 30% to 75%, and with attention deficit
disorder from 0% to 57%. There appears to be a rather intricate relationship between depression and anxiety disorders (Dwivedi, 1996a). In
fact, in about two-thirds of children with depressive disorders there is a
history of anxiety disorders preceding depression. Similarly, there are
sufficient anxiety symptoms to meet the criteria for an anxiety disorder
in some 40% of children with depressive disorders (Kovacs *et al.*, 1989).
It may indicate that anxiety predisposes children to suffer from depression and/or anxiety and depression may reflect different evolutionary
periods of the same disorder (Goodyer *et al.*, 1991).

A number of longitudinal studies (Harrington *et al.*, 1994; Kovacs *et
al.*, 1993; Myers *et al.*, 1991; Rao *et al.*, 1993) have found a strong association between childhood and adolescent depression and subsequent
suicidal behaviour in adulthood. Dysthymia is a subcategory of depression and is a disorder of chronic proportions that frequently begins in
childhood or adolescence. It has an insidious onset but later it may
develop into a major depressive disorder (Kovacs *et al.*, 1984;
Markowitz *et al.*, 1992; Angst, 1995).

Looking at the contributory factors in the genesis of depressive disorders in children and adolescents one finds a very complex interplay of
biological and environmental forces. There is often an intricate interaction between the environmental, biological and genetic factors in the
development of most disorders including depression. In a study by
Kelvin (1995) even the siblings of depressed children appeared to have
three times (that is, 42%) the reported prevalence of community
samples.

Monck *et al.* (1994) found that maternal distress and the quality of
the mother's marriage were independently associated with the presence
of depression and anxiety disorders in a sample of adolescent girls.
Goodyer *et al.* (1989) have shown that anxiety and depressive disorders
are significantly more common in those school-age children who report
moderate to poor friendships in their own lives. Children's vulnerabil-

ity to depression also increases if they have experienced abuse, parental discord or separation, and mental illness in the care givers. Children who experience persistent, prolonged or uncontained distress may thus become vulnerable to depressive disorders.

The emergence of depressive disorders can be understood in terms of emotional development. Emotions are highly specific physiological responses to particular events. Human beings, by virtue of their shared genetic heritage, are equipped with such phylogenetically adapted response packages from infancy. These patterns of emotional responses change in various ways (such as self-regulation and differentiation) in the context of maturation, development, socialization and training (Dwivedi, 1993a, 1996). The responses contain within them a propensity towards certain actions that regulate the situations that trigger them. They also have signalling properties that communicate some of one's mental state to oneself and others.

These emotional responses are influenced by cognitive processes that are subject to maturation, development and complexity. It is through these cognitive processes that incentive events are modulated, their emotional significance is assessed and modified, and the consequences of potential actions are predicted. The entire emotional response is therefore greatly influenced by cognitive processes. Similarly, emotional responses, in turn, influence the development of cognitive processes and learning. There is thus a spiralling interaction between cognition and emotion (Lewis and Miezitis, 1992).

When an infant tries to engage the parent and the parent does not respond, the infant eventually looks away from the unresponsive parent because the frustration caused by the failure to attain its goals is very distressing. The infant may eventually even give up trying (Beebe and Stern, 1977; Brazelton, 1982). Action tendencies are therefore influenced by cognitive appraisals that may make it impossible to act, thus restricting one's repertoire of responses. 'Depression constitutes a recursively shrinking repertoire in which the spiralling loop becomes narrow and constricted over time. Thus it is shaped like a cone which gets narrower and narrower' (Lewis and Miezitis, 1992, p. 43).

This constriction and inhibition of certain behaviours is also described by Sloman *et al.* (1994) in their concept of an 'involuntary subordinate strategy' (ISS). When participants take part in contests, their autonomic internal control systems become activated. Winners experience physiological changes associated with a surge in energy and confidence whereas losers experience inhibition of further challenging or assertive behaviours. Depression is therefore equivalent to a powerful ISS together with self-blame and it helps to bring aggression under control. In psychotherapy this adaptive function of depressive behaviour can be utilized to reframe the victim's behaviour as an act of self-sacrifice in order to protect others.

Knowledge and experience of the management of depressive disorders in children and adolescents have advanced substantially in recent years. A variety of approaches have constantly been refined. There has also been a growing awareness of the therapeutic effectiveness of stories, particularly with children (Dwivedi, 1996a). Many therapeutic approaches – namely psychodynamic psychotherapy, cognitive-behavioural therapy and pharmacotherapy – are presented in this volume. Their application (either on their own or in combination with other therapies) depends upon the needs of particular cases and the resources and the skills available to the helping agencies.

This volume outlines the roles of schools, primary health care and social work in this context. It is really amazing how much relief can be achieved from simple but skilled help. A recent publication by the Royal College of Psychiatrists in association with the West London Health Promotion Agency (Graham and Hughes, 1995), aimed at the parents and teachers of depressed children, outlines practical advice and information on the subject. A comprehensive resource book for professionals to help parents enhance their parenting skills is also in preparation (Dwivedi, 1997). A range of therapeutic interventions are required for the treatment and prevention of depression in young people and 'the multiple problems of the depressed young person make it especially important that multimodal approaches to treatment are used' (Harrington and Vostanis, 1995, p. 334). Unfortunately 'the pool of professionals is not sufficiently large to meet the mental health needs of our juvenile population' (Kovacs and Bastiaens, 1995, p. 304). There is an urgent need to evolve comprehensive services so that early and appropriate intervention is available (Dwivedi, 1993b). Early intervention would improve adjustment during childhood and would reduce the incidence of emotional distress and disability during adulthood. The problem now is not so much the lack of a body of therapeutic knowledge but rather the lack of the resources needed to provide assistance. Several recent surveys of child mental health services have highlighted enormous gaps between what is required and what is available (Kurtz, 1992; Kurtz et al., 1994). Parry-Jones (1992) underlines the

> ... evidence of prolonged lack of funding, resulting in marked shortfall of manpower by any standards and in poor working conditions, rendering child and adolescent psychiatry a truly 'Cinderella' service. Under such circumstances, opportunities for involvement in less urgent clinical activities, such as preventive or health promotion programmes are likely to be absent or minimal. (p. 5)

Recent official documents (NHS Health Advisory Service, 1995; Audit Commission, 1994) have also highlighted the urgent need for the creation of an appropriate infrastructure for child mental health services at primary, secondary and tertiary levels, offering a comprehensive service (that is, promotive, curative and rehabilitative services) in a collaborative fashion (involving Departments of Health, Social Services, Education, and so forth).

In Chapter 1 of this volume, Julian Brockless deals with the definition, characteristics and classification of depression in children and adolescents along with its epidemiology as well as the biological and psychological mechanisms involved. Chapter 2, by Ingrid Davison, outlines practical assessment procedures and guidelines for planning treatment, and provides a case study.

In Chapter 3, Joan Hutten outlines the social context of depression and the need to support families in stress. She also provides a detailed case illustration and discusses the role of institutions and professionals – and particularly the role of social workers in child guidance clinics – in this respect.

Biddy Youell, in Chapter 4, provides an excellent account of psychodynamic psychotherapy with the help of some interesting case examples. In Chapter 5, which deals with cognitive-behavioural therapy, Mary Evans and Ann Murphy, discuss the cognitive distortions in depression and provide an interesting account of this method of treatment. Finn Cosgrove, in Chapter 6, outlines the neurotransmitter systems involved in depression and discusses the place of medication in its management.

In Chapter 7, Muriel Barrett and Judith Waterfield focus on learning and explore how depression affects the cognitive and social skills of children and young people. They also discuss how schools and educational therapists can help such children. In Chapter 8, Graham Curtis Jenkins examines the role of primary health care in the management of depression in children and adolescents. Chapter 9, by Philip Barker, outlines the building blocks of a comprehensive service for defeating depression in children and adolescents.

References

Angold A, Costello EJ (1993) Depressive comorbidity in children and adolescent: empirical, theoretical, and methodological issues. American Journal of Psychiatry 150(12): 1779–91.

Angst J (1995) The epidemiology of dysthymia. Focus on Depression 3(3): 1–5.

Audit Commission (1994) Seen but not Heard. London: HMSO.

Beebe B, Stern, DN (1977) Engagement–disengagement and early object experiences. In Freedman M, Grand S (Eds) Communicative Structures and Psychic Structures. New York: Plenum.

Brazelton, TB (1982) Early intervention: What does it mean? In Fitzgerald HE, Lester BM, Yogman MW (Eds) Theory and Research in Behavioral Pediatrics. New York: Plenum.

Dwivedi KN (1993a) Emotional development. In Dwivedi KN (Ed) Groupwork with Children and Adolescents: A Handbook. London: Jessica Kingsley.

Dwivedi, KN (1993b) Group work in child mental health services. In Dwivedi KN (Ed) Group Work with Children and Adolescents. London: Jessica Kingsley.

Dwivedi KN (1996) Culture and personality. In Dwivedi KN, Varma VP (Eds) Meeting the Needs of Ethnic Minority Children. London: Jessica Kingsley.

Dwivedi KN (1996a) Introduction. In Dwivedi KN and Varma VP (Eds) A Handbook of Childhood Anxiety Management. Aldershot: Arena.

Dwivedi KN (Ed) (1997a in press) Therapeutic Use of Stories. London: Routledge.

Dwivedi KN (Ed) (1997b in press) Enhancing Parenting Skills. London: John Wiley & Sons.

Goodyer IM (1995) Introduction. In Forrest G (Ed) Childhood Depression. London: Association of Child Psychology and Psychiatry.

Goodyer I, Germany E, Gowrusankur J, Altham P (1991) Social influences on the course of anxious and depressive disorders in school-age children. British Journal of Psychiatry 158: 676–84.

Goodyer I, Wright C, Altham P (1989) Recent friendships in anxious and depressed school age children. Psychological Medicine 19: 165–74.

Graham P, Hughes C. (1995) So Young, So Sad, So Listen. London: Gaskel/West London Health Promotion Agency.

Harrington R, Bredenkamp D, Groothues C, Rutter M, Fudge H, Pickles A. (1994) Adult outcomes of childhood and adolescent depression, III. Links with suicidal behaviours. Journal of Child Psychology and Psychiatry 35 (7): 1309–19.

Harrington R, Vostanis P (1995) Longitudinal perspectives and affective disorders in children and adolescents. In Goodyer IM (Ed) The Depressed Child and Adolescent: Developmental and Clinical Perspectives. Cambridge: Cambridge University Press (pp. 311–41).

Kelvin RG (1995) The depressed child: impact on siblings. In Forrest G (Ed) Childhood Depression. London: Association of Child Psychology and Psychiatry.

Kovacs M, Bastiaens LJ (1995) The psychotherapeutic management of major depressive and dysthymic disorders in childhood and adolescence: issues and prospects. In Goodyer IM (Ed) The Depressed Child and Adolescent: Developmental and Clinical Perspectives. Cambridge: Cambridge University Press (pp. 281–310).

Kovacs M, Frienberg TL, Crouse-Novack MA, Paulauskas SL, Pollock M, Finkelstein R (1984) Depressive disorders in childhood: a longitudinal study of the risk for a subsequent major depression. Archives of General Psychiatry 41: 643–9.

Kovacs M, Gatsonis C, Paulauskas SL, Richards C (1989) Depressive disorders in childhood: IV. A longitudinal study of comorbidity with and risk for anxiety disorders. Archives of General Psychiatry 46: 776–82.

Kovacs M, Goldston D, Gatsonis, C (1993) Suicidal behaviors and childhood onset of depressive disorders: a longitudinal investigation. Journal of the American Academy of Child Psychiatry 32: 8–20.

Kurtz Z. (Ed) (1992) With Health in Mind: Mental Health Care for Children and Young People. London: Action for Sick Children.

Kurtz Z, Thomes R, Wolkind S (1994) Services for the Mental Health of Children and Young People in England: a National Review: Report to the Department of Health. London: South West Thames RHA.

Lewis MD, Miezitis S (1992) Emotional development and depression. In Miezitis S (Ed) Creating Alternatives to Depression in Schools. Seattle: Hogrefe & Huber Publishers.

Markowitz J, Moran ME, Kocsics JH, Frances AJ (1992) Prevalence and comorbidity of dysthymic disorder among psychiatric outpatients. Journal of Affective Disorders 24: 63–71.

Miezitis S (1992) Introduction. In Miezitis S (Ed) Creating Alternatives to Depression in Schools. Seattle: Hogrefe & Huber Publishers.

Monck E, Graham P, Richman N, Dobbs R (1994) Adolescent girls II: background factors in anxiety and depression states. British Journal of Psychiatry 165: 770–80.

Myers K, McCauley E, Calderon R, Treder R (1991) The 3 year longitudinal course of suicidality and predictive factors for subsequent suicidality in youths with major depressive disorder. Journal of the American Academy of Child Psychiatry 30: 804–10.

NHS Health Advisory Service (1995) Child and Adolescent Services: Together We Stand. London: HMSO.

Nolen-Hoeksema S, Girgus JS (1994) The emergence of gender differences in depression during adolescence. Psychological Bulletin 115(30): 424–43.

Parry-Jones W (1992) Management in the National Health Service in relation to children and their provision of child psychiatric services. ACCP Newsletter 14 (1): 3–10.

Rao U, Weissman MM, Martin JA, Hammond, RW (1993) Childhood depression and risk of suicide: preliminary report of a longitudinal study. Journal of the American Academy of Child Psychiatry 32: 21–7.

Sloman L, Price J, Gilbert P, Gardner B (1994) Adaptive function of depression: psychotherapeutic implications. American Journal of Psychotherapy 48(3): 401–16.

Weller EB, Weller RA (1990) Depressive disorders in children and adolescents. In Garfinkel BD, Carolson GA, Weller EB (Eds) Psychiatric disorders in children and adolescents. Philadelphia: WB Saunders Co.

Chapter 1
The Nature of Depression in Childhood: its Causes and Presentation

JULIAN BROCKLESS

General conceptual considerations

> 1. Depression is not an illness, but a psychobiological reaction which can be provoked in anyone.
> 2. It is much more easily provoked in some people than in others.

These words, penned by Anthony Storr, appeared in the *British Journal of Psychiatry* in 1983 (Storr, 1983) and are similar to the ideas of Arieti (1978). Despite a huge volume of research into the subject over the last decade or two, they still ring true and yet remain as enigmatic as ever: the dividing line between normality and pathology remains vague and controversial. Confusion over the nature of depression in children has tended to follow developments in the field of adult mental illness (Kendell, 1976; Grinker, 1961). Much of the debate and argument appears to concern distinguishing the observation and grouping of symptoms from the inference of supposed underlying mechanisms and causes (Philips and Friedlander, 1982).

Different meanings can be given to the term 'depression' as has been outlined by Angold (1988a) and several other authors (Pearce, 1977; Gittelman-Klein, 1977; Carlson and Cartwell, 1980). These meanings overlap to a greater or lesser extent. They are:

(a) a lowering of mood within the limits of normal experience;
(b) an emotional reaction to an adverse event such as bereavement, business failure, or desertion by spouse, sexual partner or carer;
(c) a trait found in some individuals whose mood falls in response to events that would cause little upset to others;
(d) a symptom where mood is lowered to an abnormal degree, or for an abnormal duration, or is of an abnormal type as defined by the

DSM III description of 'melancholia' ('distinct quality of depressed mood');

(e) a syndrome involving a set of symptoms occurring together in a recognizable pattern but not amounting to illness or disorder because it does not cause significant impairment of normal functioning; one example might be the 'depressive' phase of normal grieving as described by Murray Parkes (1972) in which it is not unusual to find, for a period of time, the loss of pleasure in normal activities, loss of appetite and disturbed sleep found in cases of clinically diagnosed depression;

(f) a cause of loss of normal functioning that meets the criteria set by Pearce (1977) and others for depression to be seen as a disorder rather than as a syndrome (the presence of the symptoms of a depressive syndrome to a sufficient extent to constitute 'a definitive change from ... previous personality and severe enough to cause impairment of normal functioning');

(g) an illness or disease – strictly speaking this can only be satisfactorily diagnosed if the pattern of symptoms impairs normal functioning and has recognizable antecedents that can be confidently seen as causal, plus a response to certain treatment measures.

Epidemiology and presentation

Given the difficulties that appear to be inherent in the definition of depressive disorder it is not surprising that several attempts at definition have been made (American Psychiatric Association, 1980; Spitzer *et al.*, 1978; Poznanski, 1982; Weinberg *et al.*, 1973; Pearce, 1977; Frommer, 1978; see Table 1.1). It will be seen that they are similar but are not identical – a sure recipe for misunderstandings and controversy.

There is also need for caution when gathering clinical histories and symptoms. Several research projects on the use of symptom rating scales (such as Angold *et al.*, 1987; Kazdin *et al.*, 1983) have shown that, although ratings of symptoms by given individuals (parents or children) show good consistency within raters, parents tend markedly to under-report their children's subjective feelings of depression, such as a low mood and feelings of hopelessness, helplessness and worthlessness. Boys tended to be less aware of their own feelings than girls and their reports therefore tended to correspond more with those of their parents.

None the less, Kashani and his colleagues (Kashani and Simonds, 1979; Kashani *et al.*, 1983) have investigated various large samples of children and found that about 1.8–2% of children aged 9 years met the DSM III criteria for major depression and about 2.5% met the criteria for minor depression. When depression as a 'symptom' rather than as a 'disorder' was used as a criterion, however, this figure rose to 17.4%. This accords reasonably closely with the findings of Kaplan *et al.* (1984), using the Beck Depression Inventory cut-off points, that, in a sample of 11–18 year olds, 13.5% were mildly depressed, 7.3% were moderately depressed and 1.3% were severely depressed.

All these studies are in reasonable agreement with more recent research findings on major depression, which report rates between 0.5% and 2.5% (Anderson *et al.*, 1987; Velez *et al.*, 1989), and with earlier epidemiologic studies of children, such as the Isle of Wight Study (Rutter *et al.*, 1978) which found an approximately 15% incidence of depressed mood. This study, intriguingly, produced results similar to a study of the prevalence of depressed mood in female adults by Brown and Harris (1978). In the latter study depression, which had a prevalence of around 20%, was sufficient to disturb daily functioning.

The picture is, however, complicated by gender differences which change with age. There is clear evidence of an increase in suicide and deliberate self-harm with age (Shaffer and Fisher, 1981; Hawton, 1982) and the Isle of Wight team, on reexamining the ten year olds in their initial sample at the age of 14, found large increases in both depressive disorder and depression as a symptom (Rutter, cited by Angold, 1988a). Recent findings concerning rates of major depression in adolescents show rates of 2% to 8% – higher than among children (Kashani *et al.*, 1987; Velez *et al.*, 1989; McGee *et al.*, 1990; Whitaker *et al.*, 1990; Roberts *et al.*, 1991; Cooper and Goodyer, 1993). Although the gender ratio in samples of depressed subjects is equal before the age of puberty, women are twice as likely to be depressed as men after the age of 15 (Weissman and Klerman, 1977, 1978; Amenson and Lewinsohn, 1981; Boyd and Weissman, 1981). On the other hand, one study from France (Bailly *et al.*, 1992) using DSM III R criteria, suggests that this gender difference may possibly be an artifact of Anglo-Saxon culture: it found very similar incidences of depression in male and female 17 year olds (4.1% and 4.7% respectively). The 'cultural artifact' hypothesis receives support from evidence of a secular trend towards increased rates of deliberate self-harm in the USA (Shaffer, 1988) and the UK (Hawton, 1992) and from evidence of possible increased rates of depression among children (Ryan *et al.*, 1992) and young adults (Klerman, 1988).

Some researchers have also found that depressive symptoms are more common in children and adolescents of lower socioeconomic status (Kaplan *et al.*, 1984; Schoenbach *et al.*, 1982) and in youngsters from non-white ethnic groups (Schoenbach *et al.*, 1982), whereas others (Kandel and Davies, 1982) have found no such differences, possibly illustrating the findings of Marks *et al.* (1979) that general practitioners seem to fail to diagnose depression most easily in the young and in the more highly educated.

Table 1.1: Diagnostic criteria for childhood depression

Author	Required duration of symptoms	Core symptoms	Required number of additional symptoms	Sleep, appetite, energy, retardation	Self image, suicidal thoughts cognitive functions, sociability, attitude to school	Others (e.g. somatic complaints, aggression, anxiety/phobia, obsession, regression, sphincter control)
Weinberg et al. (1973)	1 month	Low mood/self-blame and deprecation	Five	Sleep disturbance, unexpected change in appetite or weight, loss of energy	Diminished socialization, change in school performance, and attitude to school	Somatic complaints, aggressive behaviour, agitation
Pearce (1977)	4 weeks or more	Misery, sadness, tearfulness	Five	Sleep disturbance, change in appetite and/or weight	Thoughts of death or suicide, school refusal	Alimentary upset abdominal pain or general hypochondriasis, irritability, anxiety phobias, obsessions
Frommer (1978)	Not specified	Complaint of depression/weepiness/moodiness	Not specified	Initial insomnia, excessive appetite	Poor school performance, school phobia	Abdominal pain, anti-social behaviour, tension, explosiveness, hostility, anxiety, emotional immaturity or clinging to mother, enuresis and/or faecal soiling

Spitzer et al. (1978)	1 week (probable) 2 weeks (definite)	Dysphoria and/or perceived loss of pleasure	Four (probable) five (definite)	Sleep difficulty or excessive sleep, poor appetite/weight loss or increased appetite/weight gain, loss of energy, tiredness, fatigue, psychomotor agitation or retardation	Self-reproach or excessive guilt, recurrent thoughts of death or suicide, decreased ability to think or concentrate	Loss of interest in pleasure
Poznanski (1982)	1 month	Depressed mood, behaviour or appearance	Four (probable) five (definite)	Sleep difficulty, fatigue, hypoactivity	Lowered self-esteem, pathological guilt, morbid/suicidal ideation, social withdrawal, difficulty with schoolwork	'Anhedonia'
DSM-IV (APA, 1994)	At least 2 weeks	Dysphoric mood or loss of interest or pleasure in nearly all activities	Four or more	Change in sleep, appetite or weight, decrease in energy, change in psychomotor activity	Feelings of worthlessness or guilt, difficulty in thinking, concentration or decision making, recurrent thoughts of death or suicidal ideation, plans or attempts	

Other factors, such as developmental variations in the way children show depression, also complicate the picture. Of particular interest is the finding by Puig-Antich (1982) that up to a third of his depressed patients initially presented with disturbed behaviour. I have also encountered clinical situations in which depression has shown itself in teenage girls through sexual 'acting out' in the form of an avid pursuit of sexual gratification, a phenomenon I have seen more often in bereaved men, as if sexual enjoyment were being used as a compensation or distraction to counteract low mood. This phenomenon has also been noted by other writers on the subject of adolescent depression (Shafii and Shafii, 1992).

Attempts at definition

Many have attempted to define the clinical features of depressive disorder in a child (see Table 1.1; Pearce, 1977; Frommer, 1978; Weinberg *et al.*, 1973; DSM-IV, 1994; Spitzer *et al.*, 1977; Poznanski, 1982). Nearly all propose a central, core set of symptoms of lowered mood, loss of pleasure in normal activities and low self-esteem, added to impairments of normal functioning, a certain number of which must be present for diagnosis (such as sleeplessness, appetite change, morbid ideation, lowered concentration and performance at school, and agitation). There is less consensus on the number of 'non-core' symptoms and the duration of symptoms and *much* less consensus on symptomatic and behavioural 'depressive equivalents' such as somatic symptoms, aggressive behaviour, school refusal, other phobias, obsessions, clinging, wetting and soiling.

It is easy to see from the number of different sets of criteria how misunderstandings and controversy arise in the field of depression in childhood: each definition of depression is similar to, but different from, the next and, although the definitions are in all probability devised for specific research or clinical purposes, they are all too often taken as statements of fact that apply to all instances.

A further serious impediment to the definition and differentiation of depression in childhood and adolescence is the astounding rate of simultaneous comorbidity. For example, Kovacs *et al.* (1984a) found that nearly four fifths of the school-aged children with major depression in their study met diagnostic criteria for another psychiatric disorder, mostly anxiety (33%); a large overlap was also found between major depression and dysthymic disorder (DD). Ryan *et al.* (1987) found that 45% of the depressed children and 27% of the depressed adolescents in their sample had avoidant/phobic-type disorders. On the other hand, Kashani *et al.* (1987), in their sample of depressed adolescents, found high rates of oppositional and conduct disorders (75% and 50%) and of alcohol and drug abuse (25% each) in addition to simultaneous anxiety disorder in 75%. Puig-Antich (1982) found that about a third of his sample of depressed preadolescents who were being entered for a trial of treatment with imipramine met both RDC ICD 9 criteria for major depression and DSM III criteria for conduct disorder.

Subtypes of depression in children and adolescents

According to Cantwell (1983) there may be a childhood equivalent of the distinction sometimes made in adults between 'familial pure depressive disease' (FPDD) or 'primary depression', and 'depressive spectrum disease' (DSD) or 'secondary depression' (depression that is secondary to life events). The former tend to have longer, more discrete episodes whereas the latter have more variable illnesses coinciding with interpersonal difficulties; indeed, secondary depression may be more akin to 'disthymic disorder' in DSM-III. It is said to have at least two subtypes: 'characterologic' with onset below the age of 25, and 'chronic' which has a later onset.

In a follow-up study of 133 children from infancy to early adulthood, Chess (cited by McConville and Rae-Grant, 1985) identified two cases of primary depression and four of secondary. The primary depressives exhibited symptoms at an early age (8–12 years), had positive family histories, and their symptoms continued into adulthood without changing character. In contrast, the secondary depressives had negative family histories and disturbed backgrounds. Their depressive symptoms developed later (after the age of 13 years) but were preceded by symptoms of other disorders such as attention deficit and conduct problems.

An early attempt to subclassify childhood depression followed studies of depressed inpatients by McConville et al. (1973) and McConville and Rae-Grant (1985). It attempted to relate the symptoms and signs to the child's state of cognitive development. These writers divided childhood depression into 'affectual', 'negative self-esteem' and 'guilt' types.

The first is typified by onset at the age of 6–8 years, and characterized by a sense of inner loss, sadness and helplessness, and an unfocused sense of having been 'bad'. There appear to be no typical antecedents; the response to psychotherapy is reported to be 'reasonable' and the response to drugs is reported as 'unclear'.The second typically develops around the age of 8–10 years. The cognitive symptoms contain more specific feelings of incompetence in life, uselessness and worthlessness to others, and a sense that this will never change. Again, there are no apparent antecedents and the respective responses to drugs and psychotherapy are said to be 'unclear' and 'poor'.

The third subtype was not found in the sample studied by McConville and Rae-Grant below the age of 10 years. It is typified by a very strong sense of guilt, of one's own wickedness which deserves punishment, and by self-destructive thoughts that seem to have elements of both self-punishment and restitution. In the McConville and Rae-Grant study this type of depression differed from the other two types that followed a sudden, traumatic loss; its response to both drugs and psychotherapy was reported to be good. It is tempting to see it as the closest equivalent to the 'depression' phase of normal grieving.

The 'negative self-esteem' type of depression seemed the most refractory to treatment, tempting one to equate it with the 'characterologic' type of adult dysthymic disorder, with its concept of depressive tendencies somehow deeply ingrained in the personality. More recent studies by Ryan and Kolvin and their colleagues (Ryan et al., 1987; Kolvin et al., 1991) used principal components analysis and reached rather similar sets of subtypes: 'anxiety', 'negative cognition' and 'endogenous/biological'. The similarity even extends to an association of the third of these with loss events in the school years, usually the death of a loved grandparent (cf. the McConville and Rae-Grant 'guilt' type of depression). The 'negative self-esteem' and 'negative cognition' types in the two studies also appear to share symptoms of feeling worthless and useless.

Ryan et al. (1987a) also found evidence of subtypes differentiated by weight/appetite change and the presence of disturbed conduct which were not found by Kolvin and his colleagues. This disturbed conduct category possibly shares some elements with the 'characterologic' subtype of adult secondary depression mentioned earlier.

There is further evidence for a mixed conduct/depressive disorder in the work of Puig-Antich (1982) on the effects of treatment with imipramine. Some children who met the criteria for both depressive and conduct disorders improved their behaviour when adequately treated for their depression. Work by Harrington et al. (1991) on a similar sample also appears to show that, when compared to other depressed children, these patients show lower rates of depression in other family members and lower rates of depression themselves in later life when followed up into adulthood. Hughes et al. (1990) found a better response rate to imipramine among children with pure depression, or depression mixed with anxiety, than among patients in their sample with depression mixed with conduct or oppositional disorders.

McConville and Rae-Grant (1985) cite Bemporad's (1982) attempt to relate depressive subtypes to a much earlier theoretical model by Loevinger (1976), based on the psychoanalytic ideas of Erikson (1968) on the ways self-esteem can be boosted or damaged at different stages of development by supply or deprivation of the 'core need' relevant to each stage: in infancy warmth, comfort, oral stimulation and the satisfied feeling of a full stomach; mastery of bodily functions during the toddler years; at the 3–5-year-old, 'oedipal' stage the ability to elicit adult affection, especially from the parent of the opposite sex; mastery of basic life skills at primary school age; and in adolescence the attainment of adult independence and separation from the family of origin. Similar ideas have more recently been put forward by American (Shafii and Shafii, 1992) and French (Revol *et al.*, 1994) reviewers.

Table 1.2: Subtypes of depressive disorder in children

Reprinted from McConville and Rae-Grant (1985). The Diagnosis and Treatment of Depressive Subtypes in Children, pp. 128–9, with kind permission from Elsevier Science Ltd, The Boulevard, Langford Lane, Kidlington OX5 1GB

Type I Affectual depression

1. 'I feel sad/I cry' (sadness/crying).
2. 'Someone must help me/take care of me or no one will' (helplessness, hopelessness).
3. 'I feel lonely/empty inside' (withdrawal, inner loss).
4. 'I have lost people/others whom I need to care for me/look after me' (separation, nurturance concerns).
5. 'I must have been bad in some (unspecified) way/it must have been something I did' (non-specific, unfocused guilt).

Type II Negative self-esteem depression

6. 'I feel that I am no good inside/I never will be any good to myself/I am mean, stupid, punk' (self-estimate).
7. 'I am no help to others/can't do things for others/have nothing to give others' (estimate of worth to others).
8. 'No one likes/wants to like me for myself' (assumption regarding others' views).
9. 'People will use me/take advantage of me/and be unfair to me' (assumption regarding others' actions).
10. 'I will (probably) always be treated this way, I should accept it/things will always be this way' (assumption of continuity).

Type III Guilt depression

11. 'I am a bad (sinful) wicked person/others hate/must hate me' (explicit guilt).
12. 'I justly deserve to be treated this way' (punitive self-estimate).
13. 'I should be/wish to be dead' (passive self-destruction).
14. 'I should/wish to kill myself' (active self-destruction).
15. 'I want to be with the dead person/make up to him by hurting myself' (restitution).

Current ideas about depression in very young children still draw heavily on the pioneering work of Spitz (1946, 1965) and Bowlby (1980) on the protest, despair and withdrawal reaction of infants separated from their primary carers. Shafii and Shafii (1992) also attempt to integrate psychoanalytic ideas with those of Piaget (1962) on cognitive development in their concept of 'sensorimotor' depression. In this they observe general inhibition of the normal activities of infancy such as sucking at breast or bottle, social smiling and exploratory behaviour. Their comments on depression at later stages of childhood and adolescence maintain the idea of inhibition of normal activities but also emphasize the increasing importance with age of overtly dysphoric mood, and of developmental regression in fields such as language, cognitive sophistication and bladder and bowel control. For example, enuresis and soiling are mentioned as possible manifestations of depression in the nursery and early school years, as is regression to concrete thinking in adolescence. With regard to depression in the toddler years, mention is made of autoerotic behaviour as a response to depressed mood, a possible analogue of the sexual 'acting out' seen in some depressed adolescent girls and some bereaved men. Shafii and Shafii (1992) also comment on depressed toddlers' behaviour towards their transitional objects, which parallels textbook patterns of eating, sleeping and sexual behaviour in depressed adults: increasing preoccupation as mood lowers until a point is reached where all interest is suddenly lost.

Possible biological correlates or mechanisms of depression in childhood and adolescence

Although the neurotransmitter hypothesis has been current for some years, its basis appears to remain the effects found in animals given drugs which have been found clinically effective in the treatment of depression in humans. Other research on depressed subjects has concentrated on neuroendocrine mechanisms and has yielded data in the areas of cortisol, thyroid and growth hormone regulation. All these areas have been investigated in juvenile depression, as has the area of sleep EEG abnormalities. On the other hand, immunological findings on depressed and bereaved adults (reviewed by Calabrese et al., 1987), which give some indications of lymphocyte depletion in these conditions, are largely inconclusive and have not been replicated in children. There is, however, a possible link with oversecretion of glucocorticoids.

Indeed, the greatest amount of literature in the neuroendocrine field on depression is on cortisol regulation, particularly the Dexamethasone Suppression Test (DST). It was discovered in about 1980 that, in about 50% of cases, the high cortisol secretion by depressed subjects failed to be suppressed by the action on the hypothalamus and pituitary of a dose of dexamethasone which, in normal subjects, would cause cortisol levels to drop dramatically (Carroll et al., 1981)

In the 1990s a substantial body of research literature has grown detailing studies which broadly but somewhat less uniformly replicate these findings in children and adolescents. This has been helpfully reviewed by Yaylayan, Weller and Weller (1992). Unfortunately, although these studies are of great academic interest, they have so far yielded little scope for useful clinical application and the DST is largely dismissed as unhelpful (in the young) by Tyrer et al. (1991). Results from studies attempting to relate DST results to suicidality and treatment outcome have also been contradictory.

A similar situation exists regarding patterns of growth hormone secretion and its response to challenge doses of insulin and clonidine. Studies in adults (such as Sachar *et al.*, 1980; Jarrett *et al.*, 1990) have found abnormalities of growth hormone secretion in depressives, sometimes to the extent that a reduction in secretion is detectable in those with recurrent depression even between episodes. This has led others to study growth hormone secretion in depressed children and adolescents (Puig-Antich *et al.*, 1984a, b, c; Ryan *et al.*, 1994). Some results have shown a generalized reduction in growth hormone levels in depressed children, with a blunted response to the challenge posed by a dose of clonidine or an insulin-induced state of hypoglycemia, which, in normal subjects, would produce a surge of growth hormone. On the other hand, Puig-Antich *et al.* (1984b) found that, in their young, depressive subjects, growth hormone secretion during sleep was increased.

A difference between research findings in adults and those in children and adolescents occurs in the field of the thyroid stimulating hormone (TSH) response to thyrotropin releasing factor (TRH). This response, which was discovered to be reduced in some depressed adults (Loosen and Prange, 1982), was no different in depressed and control children in a study by Puig-Antich (1987), although recent findings by Sokolov *et al.* (1994) have shown abnormalities in levels of T3 and T4 in juvenile depressives.

Research findings concerning the secretion of melatonin are also contradictory. Adults with major depression appear to have a decreased secretion of melatonin at night compared with controls (Wetterburg, 1983; Beck-Friis *et al.*, 1984). This has been replicated in depressed, male 7–13 year olds, compared to same aged controls (Cavallo *et al.*, 1987). In contrast, Shafii *et al.* (1990) carried out a similar study comparing groups of 6–10 year olds with primary depression, depressive features mixed with other disorders, and other psychiatric disorders without depression; they discovered a marked increase in nighttime melatonin secretion in the first group when compared with the others. The absence of a non-disturbed control group from this study disallows any entertainment of the hypothesis that the depressed children actually had normal melatonin secretion and that the non-depressed, disturbed children were the ones who might end up depressed as adults (this might arguably follow from some retrospective studies of the childhood symptoms of adult depressives).

Findings of abnormal sleep EEG patterns in depressed adults similarly seem to have been inconsistently reflected in the results from research done on children and adolescents.

Table 1.3: Developmental stages: depressive features and their causation (Bemporad, 1982; McConville and Rae-Grant, 1985)

Developmental state	Infancy	Early childhood	Middle childhood	Late childhood	Adolescence
Freudian equivalents	Oral	Anal	Oedipal	Latency	Adolescence
Eriksonian equivalents	Trust versus mistrust	Autonomy versus shame	Initiative versus guilt	Industry versus inferiority	Identity versus identity diffusion
Developmental ego states (Loevinger, 1976)	Symbiotic/pre-social	Impulsive, opportunistic, self-protective	Conformist, superficially nice, shameful and guilty for rule-breaking	Self-awareness in relation to group, conscientious/helping, conformist	Self-evaluated standards/long-term goals and ideals, guilt for consequences
Psycho-dynamics	Loss of security/sense of well-being and of stimulation	Loss of approval	Feeling rejected and loss of gratifying activities	Inability to bear threat to parental relationship and/or to meet internalized parental ideal	Inability to separate from family and/or inability to fulfil parental ideal

Type of dysphoria	Deprivation of needed stimulation	Inhibition of the urge to gratify an emerging sense of will	Transitory crying/sadness relating directly to a depriving/frustrating situation	Depression resulting from cognitive deductions about circumstances	Depression accentuated by cognitive distortions about the finality of events
Symptoms	Protest/crying then withdrawal/despair	Clinging/inhibition	Automatic sadness in response to the immediate situation	Low self-esteem and depression	Depression with impulsivity consequent upon time distortion/exaggerated sense of urgency

In adult endogenous depression, there appears to be less slow-wave sleep, more rapid-eye-movement (REM) sleep in the early part of the night, and earlier waking (Kupfer *et al.*, 1985; Rush *et al.*, 1982).

In studies of 6–13 year olds diagnosed as having major depression by RDC ICD 9 or Weinberg (1973) criteria (Puig-Antich *et al.*, 1982; Young *et al.*, 1982) no differences were found with controls on these measures, and early rather than late insomnia is more common (Puig-Antich *et al.*, 1983a). On the other hand, Lahmeyer *et al.* (1983) and Emslie *et al.* (1987, 1990) claim to have found reduced REM latency and increased REM density in depressed juveniles compared with age-matched controls; and Puig-Antich (1983b) found similar results with a group of 28 children who had recovered fully from a previous episode of major depression.

All these inconsistent findings support, in my view, the notion that the biological components of the depressive process are not yet fully established in childhood and adolescent depression – a notion I first proposed around a decade ago (Brockless, 1986, unpublished); although the findings by Puig-Antich *et al.* (1983b) of REM sleep changes in children following recovery from a depressive episode links intriguingly with other findings (such as Kovacs *et al.*, 1984b; Rhode *et al.*, 1994) that an episode of depression in youth renders one more vulnerable to similar episodes in the future. Ryan (1992) also arrives at a similar opinion when considering the efficacy of antidepressants, response to which, he suggests, may differ at different ages (as the condition evolves), even if the condition being treated is the same through the different stages of the life-cycle.

Possible psychological mechanisms

There are three main hypotheses about how depression originates: the psychoanalytic notion of object loss (Freud, 1917; Abraham, 1927; Bibring, 1953; Bowlby, 1980), the behavioural concept of 'learned help-lessness' (Seligman, 1975; Abramson, Seligman and Teasdale, 1978; Breier *et al.*, 1987), and the cognitive model proposed by Beck (1974, 1976). All three share the idea that an individual can respond to adversity by withdrawal and inaction.

In psychoanalytic circles, it is accepted that a sense of the loss of a loved person can engender feelings of emptiness and loss of the warmth associated with the loved person, and/or it can give rise to guilt and self-blame at having caused or allowed the person's disappearance. When these feelings are adequately 'worked through' and acknowledged it is possible for the individual to adjust satisfactorily to the loss. If the process is arrested or blocked by lack of acknowledgement and valida-tion, however, feelings of emptiness, guilt and self-blame ensue, inhibiting further psychic growth and interaction with the social environment by the thought either that there is no fulfilment or pleasure to be found there or that one has somehow forfeited the right to obtain such fulfilment or pleasure.

The concept of 'learned helplessness' arose from animal experiments involving the administration of unavoidable and unpredictable electric shocks over a period of time, which resulted in the animals crouching immobile in one place and not daring to explore the environment. Some support for the notion has come from the work of Breier and colleagues (1987) on healthy human subjects exposed to unavoidable, unpleasant levels of noise. Results showed subjects' self-ratings on various negative mood indicators to be higher and neuroendocrine measures, such as cortisol levels, also showed a depressive pattern.

Several studies have shown that depressed children and adolescents hold pessimistic views of their self-worth, competence and future (McCauley et al., 1988; Meyer et al., 1989; Kendall et al., 1990). This accords with Beck's work on adults from the 1970s. The cognitive model proposes that depressed mood is secondary to negative appraisal of the self, and of one's competence and ability, although it is, of course, quite possible to argue that such cognitions may be secondary to biologically induced low mood. Lewinsohn et al. (1981) argued that biological and cognitive features of depression appear and recover together and this is supported by the work of Asarnow and Bates (1988), whereas more recent studies (such as Seligman and Peterson, 1986; Reinherz et al., 1989; Nolen-Hoeksema et al., 1992; Joiner and Barnett, 1994; Brage and Meredith, 1994; Lewinsohn et al., 1994) indicate that certain ways of interacting with others and thinking about the self, characterized by overreliance on others, a sense of rejection, globally negative self-image, readiness to blame oneself in the face of failure, greater reliance on substance use (such as cigarette smoking) and less support from friendships in some cases precede the onset of depression. The finding by Kovacs et al. (1984b) and Lewinsohn et al. (1994) that episodes of depression in youth render one vulnerable to future depression is also supported by the finding of similar characteristics in the cognitive and interpersonal functioning of young, recovered depressives studied by Puig-Antich et al. (1985b) and Rhode et al. (1994).

Causal factors

Genetic

In general, depression has long been known to be more frequent in blood relatives of depressed patients than in the population at large (Winokur, 1978) and some recent studies specifically examining child and adolescent depressive patients have tended to confirm this (Puig-

Antich *et al.*, 1989; Harrington *et al.*, 1993). Others have suggested that endogenous-type major depression with an early onset yields particularly high rates of depression in relatives, perhaps indicating a particularly high genetic loading for the condition in these individuals (McConville and Rae-Grant, 1985; Weissman *et al.*, 1984a).

Studies demonstrating a reverse link have shown high rates of depression in the children of depressed parents (Beardslee *et al.*, 1993; Weissman *et al.*, 1992). On the other hand, one of these studies (Beardslee *et al.*, 1993) and some others (Weissman *et al.*, 1984b, 1987; Radke-Yarrow *et al.*, 1992) demonstrate general non-specific increases in levels of psychiatric disorders in the children of depressed parents. It could be argued that the best evidence for a genetic basis for depression comes from Tsuang's (1978) work on the concordance of affective disorders in twins: concordance rates of 76% and 67% were found in monozygotic twins reared respectively together and apart, whereas the rate in dizygotic twins was only 19%.

Psychosocial factors

A large number of studies have looked at the psychosocial antecedents of depression in childhood and adolescence following the lead of studies in adults (Brown and Harris, 1978; Paykel *et al.*, 1980; Paykel, 1982), and inspired by the findings of Spitz (1946) and Bowlby (1980) on the effects on infants of separation from the primary carer. An early study by Caplan and Douglas (1969) indeed found a higher frequency of previous bereavement among depressed children, and adverse life events have been found to be commoner in the families of depressed toddlers (Kashani *et al.*, 1986) and in the lives of depressed 7–12 year olds (Kashani *et al.*, 1990). When the data of Caplan and Douglas were examined the other way round, however, bereavement was found to be followed by a wide range of psychiatric disorders in the bereaved children. This has been confirmed by other studies of children of depressed parents (such as Orvaschel, 1983; Beardslee *et al.*, 1983; Weissman *et al.*, 1986).

Another study by Goodyer *et al.* (1993) suggests a link between recent adverse life events and depression in adolescent girls, especially when the subjects' mothers have themselves suffered from depression. The author, however, admits that the data are unable to rule out the possibility of non-specific effects both causing and arising from psychiatric disorder in general, especially as many of the depressed girls' mothers suffered psychiatric disorders other than depression.

A study by Black and Urbanowicz (1986) on proactive family intervention with bereaved children showed benefits which spanned the whole spectrum of psychiatric disorders, rather than on rates of depression alone.

A similar picture emerges from studies of the effects of parental divorce on children (Wallerstein and Kelly, 1980; Hetherington *et al.*, 1982; Wallerstein, 1983). Where depression occurs, however, much in these data points to depression as following less from the event itself than from the deficient parenting and conflict between the parents before and after the divorce. Indeed, later work on adults by Brown and his colleagues (1986) supports this by suggesting that, in those individuals suffering depression after the death of a parent, the depression is a consequence of the deficient parenting which followed the bereavement more than a result of the bereavement itself.

Two very clear antecedents of depression in children appear to be long-term illness and previous episodes of depression. Studies from several fields have shown that children can become depressed following procedures as diverse as bone fracture operations (Kashani *et al.*, 1981) and tonsillectomy (Klausner *et al.*, 1995). Depression is also seen to result from chronic malignancy, especially if hospitalization is involved and if the illness is accompanied by maternal depression (Mulhern *et al.*, 1992). Pfefferbaum-Levine *et al.* (1983) have even suggested the use of antidepressants as a useful adjunct to the treatment of children with malignant disease.

In the study by Berney *et al.* (1991), illness was one of only two factors definitely associated with depression in children. The other was a change in social relationships, such as a sudden loss or rejection by a peer group.

On the other hand, Oler *et al.* (1994) have found that adolescents who participate in athletic sports appear to be at lower risk of depression, suicidal ideation and substance abuse. One is tempted to speculate that such participation gives both the physiological protection against low mood reported to result from vigorous exercise and the social protection from loneliness and rejection inherent in being accepted and working as a member of a team.

Other factors associated with low self-esteem and depression in children, but also possibly with non-depressive psychiatric pathology, include family levels of expressed emotion (Asarnow *et al.*, 1994) and affectively charged negative statements by currently or formerly depressed mothers (Goodman *et al.*, 1994).

The proposition that low self-esteem leads to depression has *prima facie* validity, but is also confirmed by recent work by Brage and Meredith (1994) which stressed the importance of loneliness causing depression. Turner and Cole (1994) have also studied the interaction between stressful events and developmental changes in the cognitive style in which they are appraised in relation to the self: certain classes of stressful event appeared to cause negative self-appraisal only later in childhood.

A study by Rodgers (1994) suggests that depression results from an interaction between the childhood experience of parental divorce, gender, and experience of intimate relationships in adult life, there being a relationship between parental divorce in childhood and depressive symptoms in those women (not men) who had never married or who had experienced marital breakdown, but not in women in their first marriages. This implies that the negative self-appraisal leading to depression results only from an interaction between adverse life events in adulthood and earlier experiences. Indeed, there is some evidence to suggest that, in childhood, loss of a parent is more likely to be followed by a non-depressive psychiatric disorder (Rutter, 1966; Lewinsohn *et al.*, 1994). This is apparently in contradiction to the data of McConville and Rae-Grant (1985) and Berney *et al.* (1991) linking the 'endogenous' subtype of depression to recent, sudden, traumatic loss. How this affects future self-appraisal in adult life is not yet clear.

The nature of depression in children and adolescents

Much has been written on the links between depression in childhood and adulthood. The adult consequences of childhood depression and the childhood antecedents of adult depression seem equally varied (Nissen, 1971; Zeitlin, 1972) although similar variation has also been found in the antecedents of childhood depression (Kovacs *et al.*, 1984a). Chess (cited by Cantwell, 1983) found clear continuity of symptoms in two individuals, and Poznanski *et al.* (1976) found 50% continuity of depression in a sample of depressed children followed up for 6.5 years, where the symptoms became increasingly similar to those of adult-type depression over time, especially in adolescence.

Kovacs *et al.* (1989a, b) compared the histories of adjustment disorder with depressed mood (ADDM), dysthymic disorder (DD) and major depressive disorder (MDD) in a sample of 65 children.

Adjustment disorder with depressed mood and MDD both remitted more quickly, independently of the treatment, than did DD. Major depressive disorder appeared to occur only after the age of eight; whereas rates of recovery were proportional to age at onset in DD and MDD. A previous or current episode of MDD or current DD greatly increased the likelihood, and decreased the interval before a subsequent episode, of MDD; but when MDD occurred with DD this appeared not to delay recovery from DD.

Further support for Kovacs' ideas comes from more recent research by Lewinsohn and colleagues (1994) which showed that the earlier the onset of adolescent depression, the greater the likelihood of suicidal ideation, of a long rather than a brief episode, and of future recurrence, although this could also be linked to genetic studies which show earlier onset of depression in those with a strong family history.

At the more severe end of the spectrum of adult depressive disorder, it is relatively easy to see the symptoms of delusional guilt, morbid self-blame, psychomotor retardation, anorexia, early waking and diurnal variation of mood as an illness requiring medical treatment because the good response to ECT and antidepressant drugs is well known. When such a condition responds easily to these treatments it quite readily fits the disease or medical model based on germ theory of illness as a qualitative change in function with a well-defined single cause, the removal of which effects cure. In this case the putative cause is a drop in the level of certain neurotransmitters in certain synaptic clefts, a fault cured by blocking their reuptake or metabolism.

Research on the origins of depression, especially the less severe types found in community samples, has, however, found the following factors to be important: adverse life events (Paykel et al., 1969), poor living conditions, burdensome parental responsibilities such as having a handicapped child or children (Gath, 1978; Byrne and Cunningham, 1985), lack of a confiding relationship and, most important, childhood experience of parental divorce (Wallerstein and Kelly, 1980; Rodgers, 1994) and early bereavement (Brown and Harris, 1978; Caplan and Douglas, 1969), although later work by one of these teams (Brown, Harris and Bifulco, 1986) indicates that it is not so much the early loss of the mother per se which seems to produce vulnerability to depression but rather the deficits in parental care that follow.

It is my own opinion both that these factors are indeed operative and that depression in adult life can appear solely as a result of spontaneous neurochemical changes following a process in which the biological component of a person's reaction to adversity becomes independent from its precipitating psychosocial cause. There is possibly some support for this from the results of research by Kovacs and her team (Kovacs et al., 1984b) which showed that, even in children with depression, one episode may render the patient more vulnerable to further episodes than would otherwise be the case. Other research has shown significant psychosocial disablement following depression in youth (Puig-Antich et al., 1985b; Rhode et al., 1994) and a link between childhood depression and suicide in adulthood mediated by a link between childhood and adult depression (Harrington et al., 1994). Nevertheless, I still strongly agree with Storr's (1983) caution against accepting a watertight distinction between 'reactive' and 'endogenous' depression because precipitating factors in a given episode may not always be apparent at presentation.

It is also my opinion that the 'medical' model of depression is much less readily applicable to children and adolescents than to adults because the young age of these patients means that they are not so likely to have progressed down the line leading from psychosocial to neurochemical precipitation of episodes. There is some support for this from the lack of a clear demonstration by research findings that drug treatment is of any benefit in childhood and adolescent depression (Jensen *et al.*, 1992), although in the same journal Conners (1992) and Strober (1992) have put forward methodological reasons for caution in writing off antidepressants as a useful treatment in the young. Indeed, some researchers (Puig-Antich *et al.*, 1980; Puig-Antich, 1982, 1987; Kashani *et al.*, 1984) found considerable variation in response to antidepressants depending on factors such as drug plasma levels and symptom profile. On the other hand, McConville and Rae-Grant (1985), found that the subtypes of childhood depression that responded best to drug treatment also responded best to psychosocial interventions. Certainly, my own clinical experience has been that many children and teenagers showing severe, endogenous-type depressive symptoms such as anhedonia, anorexia, weight loss and early waking, who have refused drug treatment, or who had it refused on their behalf by parents, often show quite quick resolution of these clinical features in response to good compliance by parents with a structural family therapy intervention or other psychosocial management.

References

Abraham K (1927) A short study of the development of the libido viewed in the light of mental disorders. In Selected Papers of Karl Abraham. London: Hogarth Press.

Abramson LY, Seligman MEP, Teasdale JD (1978) Learned helplessness in humans: critique and reformulation. Journal of Abnormal Psychology 87: 49–74.

Amenson CS, Lewinsohn PM (1981) An investigation into the observed sex difference in prevalence of unipolar depression. Journal of Abnormal Psychology 90: 1–13.

Anderson JC, Williams S, McGee R, Silva PA (1987) 'DSM III disorders in preadolescent children: Prevalance in a large sample from the general population. Archives of General Psychiatry 44: 69–76.

Angold A (1988a) Childhood and adolescent depression, I: Epidemiological and aetiological aspects. British Journal of Psychiatry 152: 601–17.

Angold A, Weissman MM, John K, Merikangas KR, Prusoff BA, Wickramaratre P, Davis-Gammon, G. and Waner V (1987) Parent and child reports of depressive symptoms. Journal of Child Psychology and Psychiatry 28: 901–15.

Arieti S. (1978) The psychobiology of sadness. In Arieti S and Bemporad JR (Eds) Severe and Mild Depression. New York: Basic Books.

Asarnow JR, Bates S (1988) Depression in child psychiatric inpatients: cognitive and attributional patterns. Journal of Abnormal Child Psychology 16: 601–15.

Asarnow JR, Tompson M, Hamilton EB, Goldstein MJ, Guthrie, O (1994) Family-expressed emotion, childhood-onset depression and childhood-onset schizophrenic spectrum disorders: is expressed emotion a non-specific correlate of child psychopathology or a specific risk factor for depression? Journal of Abnormal Child Psychology 22 (2): 129–46.

Bailly D, Beuscart R, Collinet C, Alexandre JY, Parquet PhJ (1992) Sex differences in the manifestations of depression in young people: a study of French high school students. Part I: prevalence and clinical data. European Child and Adolescent Psychiatry 1 (3): 135–45.

Beardslee WR, Bemporad J, Keller MB and Klerman GL (1983) Children of parents with major affective disorder: a review. American Journal of Psychiatry 140: 825–32.

Beck AT (1974) The development of depression: a cognitive model. In Friedman RJ, Katz MM (Eds) The Psychology of Depression: Contemporary Theory and Research. New York: John Wiley.

Beck AT (1976) Cognitive therapy and the emotional disorders. New York: International University Press.

Beck-Friis J, Von Rosen D, Kjellman BF, Ljunggren JG, Wetteberg L (1984) Melatonin in relation to body measures, sex, age, season, and the use of drugs in patients with major depressive disorder and healthy subjects. Psychoneuroendocrinology 10: 261–77.

Bemporad JR (1982) Childhood depression from a developmental perspective. In Grinspoon L, Psychiatry 1982: Annual Review. Part III: Depression in Childhood and Adolescence 17: 272–82. Washington DC: American Psychiatric Association.

Berney TP, Bhate SR, Kohin I Famuyiwa OO, Barrett ML, Fundudis T, Tyrer S (1991) The context of childhood depression. British Journal of Psychiatry 159 (suppl. 11): 28–35.

Bibring E (1953) Affective disorders: the mechanisms of depression. New York: International University Press.

Black D, Urbanowicz MA (1986) Family intervention with bereaved children. Journal of Child Psychology and Psychiatry 28: 467–76.

Bowlby J (1980) Loss: sadness and depression. In Attachment and Loss. London: Hogarth Press.

Boyd JH, Weissman MM (1981) Epidemiology of affective disorders: a reexamination and future directions. Archives of General Psychiatry 38: 1039–46.

Brage D, Meredith W (1994) A causal model of adolescent depression. Journal of Psychology 128 (4): 455–68.

Breier A, Albus M, Pikar D, Zahn TP, Wolkowitz OM, Paul SM (1987) Controllable and uncontrollable stress in humans: alterations in mood and neuroendocrine and psychobiological function. American Journal of Psychiatry 144: 1419–25.

Brockless JBP (1986) Depression in childhood – current thoughts. EGO (Bulletin of the Division of Psychiatry, Unital Medical and Dental Schools, Guy's Campus) 9: 3–25.

Brown G, Harris T (1978) The social origins of depression ... . London: Tavistock Publications.

Brown GW, Harris TO, Bifulco A (1986) Long term effects of early loss of parent. In Rutter M, Izard CE, Read PB (Eds) Depression in Young People: Clinical and Developmental Perspectives 251–96. New York: Guilford Press.

Byrne EA, Cunningham CC (1985) The effects of mentally handicapped children on families: a conceptual review. Journal of Child Psychology and Psychiatry 26 (6): 857–64.

Calabrese JR, Kling MA, Gold PW (1987) Alterations in immunocompetence during stress, bereavement and depression ... . American Journal of Psychiatry 144, 1123–34.

Cantwell DP (1983) Overview of aetiologic factors. In Cantwell DP and Carlson GA (Eds) Affective Disorders Childhood and Adolescence: an Update. Lancaster, UK: MTP Press.

Caplan MG, Douglas VI (1969) Incidence of parental loss in children with depressed mood. Journal of Child Psychology and Psychiatry 10: 225–32.

Carlson GA, Cantwell OPC (1980) A survey of depressive symptoms, syndrome and disorder in a child psychiatric population. Journal of Child Psychology and Psychiatry 21: 19–25.

Carroll BJ, Feinberg M, Greden JF, Tarika J, Albala AA, Haskett RF, James NM, Kronfol Z, Lohr N, Steiner M, de Vigne JP, Young E (1981) A specific laboratory test for the diagnosis of melancholia. Archives of General Psychiatry 38: 15–22.

Cavallo A, Holt K, Hejazi MS, Richards GE, Meyer WJ (1987) Melatonin circadian rhythm in childhood depression. Journal of the American Academy of Child and Adolescent Psychiatry 26(3): 395–99.

Conners CK (1992) Methodology of antidepressant drug trials for treating depression in adolescents. Journal of Child and Adolescent Psychopharmacology 2(1): 11–22.

Cooper PJ, Goodyer IM (1993) A community study of depression in adolescent girls, I: estimates of symptom and syndrome prevalence. British Journal of Psychiatry 163: 369–74.

Diagnostic and Statistical Manual of Mental Disorder (Fourth Edition) (1994). Washington DC: American Psychiatric Association.

Emslie GJ, Roffwarg HP, Rush AJ, Weinberg WA, Parkin-Feigenhaum L (1987) Sleep EEG findings in depressed children and adolescents. American Journal of Psychiatry 144: 668–70.

Emslie GJ, Rush AJ, Weinberg WA, Rintelmann JW, Roffwarg HP (1990) Children with major depression show reduced rapid eye movement latencies. Archives of General Psychiatry 47: 119–124.

Erikson E (1968) Identity, Youth and Crisis. New York: Norton & Co.

Freud S (1917) Mourning and melancholia. In Strachey J (Ed) (1968) The Complete Psychological Works of Sigmund Freud. London: Hogarth Press.

Frommer EA (1978) Depressive illness in childhood. British Journal of Psychiatry (special issue): 117–36.

Gath A (1978) Down's Syndrome and the Family: the Early Years. London: Academic Press.

Gittelman-Klein R (1977) Definitional and methodological issues concerning depressive illness in children. In Schultenbrandt JG, Raskin A (Eds) Depression in Childhood: Diagnosis, Treatment and Conceptual Models. New York: Raven Press.

Goodman SH, Adamson LB, Riniti J, Cole S (1994) Mothers' expressed attitudes: associations with maternal depression and children's self-esteem and psychopathology. Journal of the American Academy of Child and Adolescent Psychiatry 33 (9): 1265–74.

Goodyer M, Cooper PJ, Vize CM, Ashby L (1993) Depression in 11–16-year-old girls: the role of past parental psychopathology and exposure to recent life events. Journal of Child Psychology and Psychiatry 34 (7): 1103–16.

Grinker RR (1961) Phenomena of Depression. New York: Paul B Hoeber Inc.

Harrington RC, Fudge H, Rutter M, Pickles A, Hill J (1991) Adult outcomes of childhood and adolescent depression, II: risk for antisocial disorders. Journal of the American Academy of Child and Adolescent Psychiatry 30: 434–39.

Harrington RC, Fudge H, Rutter M, Bredenkamp D, Groothues C, Pridham J (1993) Child and adult depression: a test of continuities with data from a family study. British Journal of Psychiatry 162: 627–33.

Hawton K (1982) Attempted suicide in children. Journal of Child Psychology and Psychiatry 23: 497–503.

Hawton K (1992) By their own young hand. British Medical Journal 304: 1000.

Hetherington EM, Cox M, Cox R (1982) Effects of divorce on parents and children. In Lamb ME (Ed) Non-traditional Families. Hillside, NJ: Lawrence Erlbaum.

Hughes CW, Preskorn SH, Weller E, Weller R, Hassanein R, Tucker S (1990) The effect of concomitant disorders in childhood depression on predicting treatment response. Psychopharmacology Bulletin 26 (2): 235–38.

Jarrett, DB, Miewald JM, Kupfer DJ (1990) Recurrent depression is associated with a persistent reduction in sleep-related growth hormone secretion. Archives of General Psychiatry 47: 113–18.

Jensen PS, Ryan ND, Prien R (1992) Psychopharmacology of child and adolescent major depression: present status and future directions. Journal of Child and Adolescent Psychopharmacology 2 (1): 31–45.

Joiner TE, Barnett J (1994) A test of interpersonal theory of depression in children and adolescents using a projective technique. Journal of Abnormal Child Psychology 23 (5): 595–609.

Kandel DB, Davies M (1982) Epidemiology of depressive mood in adolescents: an empirical study. Archives of General Psychiatry 39: 1205-121.

Kaplan SL, Hong GK, Weinhold C (1984) Epidemiology of depressive symptomatology in adolescents. Journal of the American Academy of Child Psychiatry 23 (1): 91–8.

Kashani JH, Simonds, JF (1979) The incidence of depression in children. American Journal of Psychiatry 136: 1203–5.

Kashani JH, Carlson GA, Beck NC, Hooper EW, Corcaran CM, McAllister JA, Fallati C, Rosenberg TK, Reid JC (1987) Depression, depressive symptoms and depressed mood among a community sample of adolescents. American Journal of Psychiatry 144: 932–4.

Kashani JH, Dandery AC, Reid JC (1990) Life events and depression in an inpatient sample. Comprehensive Psychiatry 31, 266–74.

Kashani JH, Holcomb WR, Orvaschel H (1986) Depression and depressive symptomatology in preschool children from the general population. American Journal of Psychiatry 143: 1138–43.

Kashani JH, McGee RO, Clarkson SE, Anderson JC, Walton LA, Williams S, Silva PA, Robbins AJ, Cytryn L, McKnew DH (1983) Depression in a sample of 9-year-old children. Archives of General Psychiatry 40: 1217–23.

Kashani JH, Shekim WO, Reid JC (1984) Amitriplyline in children with major depressive disorder: a double-blind, crossover, pilot study. Journal of the American Academy of Child Psychiatry 23 (34): 348–51.

Kashani JH, Venzke R, Millar EA (1981) Depression in children admitted to hospital for orthopaedic procedures. British Journal of Psychiatry 138: 21–5.

Kazdin AE, French NH, Unis AS, Esveldt-Dawson K (1983) Assessment of childhood depression: correspondence of child and parent ratings. Journal of the American Academy of Child Psychiatry 22 (2): 157–64.

Kendall PC, Stark KD, Adam T (1990) Cognitive deficit or cognitive distortion in childhood depression. Journal of Abnormal Psychology 18: 255–70.

Kendall RE (1976) The classification of depressions: a review of contemporary confusion. British Journal of Psychiatry 129: 15–28.

Klausner RD, Tom LWC, Schindler PD, Potsic WP (1995) Depression in children after tonsillectomy. Archives of Otolaryngology and Head and Neck Surgery 121: 105–8.

Klerman, GL (1988) The current age of youthful melancholia: evidence for an increase in depression in adolescents and young adults. British Journal of Psychiatry 152: 4–14.

Kolvin I, Barrett ML, Bhate SR, Berney TP, Famuyiwa OO, Fundudis T, Tyrer S (1991) The Newcastle child depression project: diagnosis and classification of depression. British Journal of Psychiatry 159 (suppl. 11): 9–21.

Kovacs M, Feinberg TL, Crouse-Novak MA, Paulouskas SL, Finkelstein R (1984a) Depressive disorders in childhood, I: a longitudinal, prospective study of characteristics and recovery. Archives of General Psychiatry 41: 229–37.

Kovacs M, Feinberg TL, Crouse-Novak MA (1984b) Depressive disorders in childhood, II: a longitudinal study of the risk for a subsequent major depression. Archives of General Psychiatry 41: 643–9.

Kupfer DJ, Ulrich RF, Coble RA, Jarrett DB, Groehocinski VJ, Doman J, Mathews G, Burbély AA (1985) Electroencephalographic sleep of young depressives. Archives of General Psychiatry 42: 806–10.

Lahmeyer HW, Poznanski EO, Bellow SN (1983) Sleep in depressed adolescents. American Journal of Psychiatry 140: 1150–3.

Lewinsohn PM, Clarke GN, Seeley JR, Rhode P (1994) Major depression in community adolescents: age at onset, episode duration and time to recurrence. Journal of the American Academy of Child and Adolescent Psychiatry 33 (6): 809–18.

Lewinsohn PM, Steinmetz JL, Larson DW, Franklin F (1981) Depression-related cognitions: antecedent or consequence? Journal of Abnormal Psychology 90 (3): 213–19.

Loevinger J (1976) Ego Development. San Francisco: Jossey-Bass.

Loosen PT, Prange AJ Jr (1982) The serum thyrotropin response to thyrotropin releasing hormone in depression: a review. American Journal of Psychiatry 139: 405–16.

Marks JN, Goldberg D, Hillier VF (1979) Determinants of the ability of general practitioners to detect psychiatric illness. Psychological Medicine 9: 337–53.

McCauley E, Mitchell JR, Burke P, Moss S (1988) Cognitive attributes of depression in children and adolescents. Journal of Consulting and Clinical Psychology 56: 903–8.

McConville B, Rae-Grant D (1985) The diagnosis and treatment of depressive subtypes in children. In Stevenson JE (Ed) Recent Research in Developmental Psychopathology. Oxford: Pergamon Press.

McConville B, Boag L, Purohit A (1973) Three types of childhood depression. Canadian Psychiatric Association Journal 18: 133–8.

McGee R, Feehan M, Williams S, Partridge F, Silva PA, Kelly J (1990) DSM III disorders in a large sample of adolescents. Journal of the American Academy of Child Psychiatry 29: 611–19.

Meyer NE, Dyck DG, Petrinack RJ (1989) Cognitive appraisal and attributional correlates of depressive symptoms in children. Journal of Abnormal Child Psychology 17, 325–36.

Mulhern RK, Fairclough DJ, Smith B, Douglas SM (1992) Maternal depression, assessment methods, and physical symptoms affect estimates of depressive symptomatology among children with cancer. Journal of Paediatric Psychology 17 (3): 313–26.

Nissen G (1971) Symptomatik und prognose depressive Verstimmungszustande in Kindes und Jungenadulter. Proceedings of the 4th European Congress 501–509.

Nolen-Hoeksema S, Girgus JS, Seligman MEP (1992) Predictors and consequence of childhood depressive symptoms … . Journal of Abnormal Child Psychology 101: 405–22.

Oler MJ, Mainous AG (III), Martin CA, Richardson E, Hamey A, Wilson D, Adams T (1994) Depression, suicidal ideation and substance abuse among adolescents. Are athletes less at risk? Archives of Family Medicine 3 (9): 781–5.

Orvaschel H (1983) Parental depression and child psychology. In Guze SB, Earls FJ, Barrett JE (Eds) Child Psychopathology and Development. New York: Raven Press.

Parkes CM (1972) Bereavement: Studies of Grief in Adult Life. London: Tavistock Publications.

Paykel, ES (1982) Life events and early environment. In Paykel ES (Ed) Handbook of Affective Disorders. New York: Guilford Press.

Paykel, ES, Emms ES, Fletcher J, Rassaby ES (1980) Life events and social support of puerperal depression. British Journal of Psychiatry 136: 339–46.

Paykel ES, Myers JK, Dienelt MN (1969) Life events and depression. Archives of General Psychiatry 21: 753–60.

Pearce JB (1977) Depressive disorder in childhood. Journal of Child Psychology and Psychiatry 18: 79–82.

Pfefferbaum-Levine, B, Kumar K, Cangir, A, Choroszy M, Roseberry EA (1983) Tricyclic antidepressants for children with cancer. American Journal of Psychiatry 140: 1074–6.

Philips I, Friedlander S (1982) Conceptual problems in the study of depression in childhood. In Grinspoon L (1982) Psychiatry 1982: Annual Review, Part III: Depression in Childhood and Adolescence. Washington DC: American Psychiatric Association.

Piaget J (1962) The stages of the intellectual development of the child. Bulletin of the Menninger Clinic 26: 120–8.

Poznanski EO (1982) The clinical characteristics of childhood depression. In Grinspoon L (Ed) Psychiatry 1982: Annual Review, Part III: Depression in Childhood and Adolescence. Washington DC: American Psychiatric Association.

Poznanski EO, Krakeneuhl V, Zrull JP (1976) Childhood depression – a longitudinal perspective. Journal of the American Academy of Child Psychiatry 15: 491–501.

Puig-Antich J (1982) Major depression and conduct disorder in prepuberty. Journal of the American Academy of Child Psychiatry 21 (2): 118–28.

Puig-Antich J (1987) Affective disorder in children and adolescents: diagnosis, validity and psychobiology. In Meltzer HY (Ed) Psychopharmacology: the Third Generation of Progress. New York: Raven Press.

Puig-Antich J, Chambers WJ, Tabrizi MA (1983) The clinical assessment of current depressive episodes in children and adolescents: interviews with parents and children. In Cantwell DP, Carlsson GA (Eds) Affective Disorders in Childhood and Adolescence – an update. Lancaster, UK: MTP Press.

Puig-Antich J, Goetz D, Davies M, Kaplan T, Davies S, Ostrow L, Asris L, Twomey J, Iyengar S, Ryan ND (1989) A controlled family history of prepubertal major depressive disorder. Archives of General Psychiatry 46, 406–18.

Puig-Antich J, Goetz R, Davies M, Fein M, Hanlon C, Chambers WJ, Tabrizi MA, Sachar EJ, Weitzman ED (1984b) Growth hormone secretion in prepubertal children with major depression, II ... . Archives of General Psychiatry 41: 463–6.

Puig-Antich J, Goetz R, Davies M, Tabrizi MA, Noracenko H, Hanlon C, Sachar EJ, Weitzman ED (1984c) Growth hormone secretion in prepubertal children with major depression IV ... Archives of Gencral Psychiatry 41: 479–83.

Puig-Antich J, Goetz R, Hanlon C, Davies M, Thompson J, Chambers WJ, Tabrizi MA, Weitzman ED (1982) Sleep architecture and REM sleep measures in prepubertal children with major depression: a controlled study. Archives of General Psychiatry 39: 932–9.

Puig-Antich J, Lukens E, Davies M, Goetz D, Brennan-Quattrock J, Todak G (1985b) Psychosocial functioning in prepubertal major depressive disorders II: interpersonal relationships after sustained recovery from affective episode. Archives of General Psychiatry 42: 511–17.

Puig-Antich J, Novacenko H, Davies M, Chambers WJ, Tabrizi MA, Krawlec V, Ambrosini PJ, Sachar EJ (1984a) Growth hormone secretion in prepubertal children with major depression I ... . Archives of General Psychiatry 41: 455–60.

Puig-Antich J, Perel JM, Chambers WJ (1980) Imipramine treatment of prepubertal major depressive disorders: plasma levels and clinical response – preliminary report. Psychopharmacology Bulletin 16 (1): 25–7.

Puig-Antich J, Goetz R, Hanlon C, Tabrizi MA, Davies M, Weitzman ED (1983b) Sleep architecture and REM sleep measures in pre-pubertal major depressives: studies during recovery from the depressive episode in a drug-free state. Archives of General Psychiatry 40: 187–92.

Radke-Yarrow M, Nottelman E, Martinez P, Fox MB, Belmont B (1992) Young children of affectively ill parents: a longitudinal study of psychosocial development. Journal of the American Academy of Child and Adolescent Psychiatry 31: 68–77.

Reinherz HZ, Stewart-Berghauer G, Pakiz B, Frost AK, Moeykens BA, Holmes WM (1989) The relationship of early risk and current mediators to depressive symptomatology in adolescence. Journal of the American Academy of Child and Adolescent Psychiatry 28: 942–7.

Revol O, Rochet T, Maillet J, Gérard D, de Villard R (1994) La dépression de l'enfant. Aspects étiologiques, cliniques et thérapeutiques. Archives Pédiatriques 1, 602–10.

Rhode P, Lewinsohn PM, Seeley JR (1994) Are adolescents changed by an episode of major depression? Journal of the American Academy of Child and Adolescent Psychiatry 33 (9): 1289–98.

Roberts RE, Lewinsohn PM, Seeley JR (1991) Screening for adolescent depression: a comparison of depression scales. Journal of the American Academy of Child and Adolescent Psychiatry 30: 58–66.

Rodgers B (1994) Pathways between parental divorce and adult depression. Journal of Child Psychology and Psychiatry 35 (7): 1289–308.

Rush AJ, Giles DE, Roffwarg HP, Parker CR (1982) Sleep EEG and dexamethasone suppression test findings in outpatients with unipolar major depressive disorders. Biological Psychiatry 17: 327–41.

Rutter M (1966) Children of sick parents: an environmental and psychiatric study (Institute of Psychiatry Maudsley Monograph). London: Oxford University Press.

Rutter M, Tizard J, Yule W, Graham P, Whitmore K (1976) Isle of Wight studies 1964–1974. Psychological Medicine 6: 313–32.

Ryan ND (1992) The pharmacologic treatment of child and adolescent depression. Psychiatric Clinics of North America 15 (1): 29–40.

Ryan ND, Dahl RE, Birmaher B, Williamson DE, Iyengar S, Nelson B, Puig-Antich J, Perel JM (1994) Stimulatory tests of growth hormone secretion in prepubertal major depression: depressed vs. normal children. Journal of the American Academy of Child and Adolescent Psychiatry 33 (6): 824–33.

Ryan ND, Puig-Antich J, Ambrosini P, Rubinovich H, Robinson D, Nelson B, Iyengar S, Twomey J (1987) The clinical picture of major depression in children and adolescents. Archives of General Psychiatry 44: 854–61.

Ryan ND, Williamson DE, Iyengar S, Orvaschel H, Reich T, Dahl RE, Puig-Antich J (1992) A secular increase in child and adolescent onset affective disorder. Journal of the American Academy of Child and Adolescent Psychiatry 31: 600–5.

Sachar EJ, Asnis G, Halbreich U, Nathan RS, Halpern F (1980) Recent studies in the neuroendocrinology of major depressive disorders ... Psychiatric Clinics of North America 3 (2), 313–27.

Schoenbach, VJ, Kaplan BH, Grimson RC, Wagner EH (1982) Use of a symptom scale to study the prevalence of a depressive syndrome in young adolescents. American Journal of Epidemiology 116: 791–800.

Seligman, MEP (1975) Helplessness: On Depression, Development and Death. San Francisco: WH Freeman & Co.

Seligman MEP, Peterson C (1986) A learned helplessness perspective on childhood depression: theory and research. In Rutter M, Izard C, Read P (Eds) Depression in Young People: Issues and Perspectives. New York: Guilford Press.

Shaffer D (1988) The epidemiology of teen suicide: an examination of risk factors. Journal of Clinical Psychiatry 9 (suppl.): 36–41.

Shaffer D, Fisher P (1981) The epidemiology of suicide in children and young adolescents. Journal of the American Academy of Child Psychiatry 20: 545–65.

Shafii M, Shafii SL (1992) Clinical manifestations and developmental psychopathology of depression. In Shafii M, Shafii SL (Eds) Clinical Guide to Depression in Children and Adolescents. Washington DC: American Psychiatric Press Inc.

Shafii M, Foster MB, Greenberg RA, McCue DA, Key MP (1990) The pineal gland and depressive disorders in children and adolescents. In Shafii M, Shafii SL (Eds) Biological Rhythms, Mood Disorders, Light Therapy and the Pineal Gland. Washington DC: American Psychiatric Press.

Sokolov ST, Kutcher SP, Joffe RT (1994) Basal thyroid indices in adolescent depression and bipolar disorder. Journal of the American Academy of Child and Adolescent Psychiatry 33 (4): 469–75.

Spitz RA (1946) Anaditic depressions: an inquiry into the genesis of psychiatric conditions in early childhood, II. Psychoanalytic Study of the Child 2: 313–42.

Spitz RA (1965) The First Year of Life. New York: International University Press.

Spitzer RL, Endicott J, Robins E (1977) Research Diagnostic Criteria (RDC) for a Selected Group of Functional Disorders. Third edition. New York: New York State Psychiatric Institute.

Storr A (1983) A psychotherapist looks at depression. British Journal of Psychiatry 143: 431–5.

Strober M (1992) The pharmacotherapy of depressive illness in adolescence III: diagnostic and conceptual issues in studies of tricyclic antidepressants. Journal of Child and Adolescent Psychopharmacology 2 (1): 23–30.

Tsuang MT (1978) Genetic counselling for psychiatric patients and their families. American Journal of Psychiatry 135: 1465–75.

Turner JE, Cole DA (1994) Developmental differences in cognitive diatheses for child depression. Journal of Abnormal Child Psychology 22 (1): 15–32.

Tyrer P, Barrett ML, Berney TP, Bhute S, Watson MJ, Fundudis T, Kolvin I (1991) The dexamethasone suppression test in children: lack of an association with diagnosis. British Journal of Psychiatry 159 (suppl.): 41–8.

Velez CN, Johnson J, Cohen P (1989) A longitudinal analysis of selected risk factors for childhood psychopathology. Journal of the American Academy of Child Psychiatry 28: 861–4.

Wallerstein JS (1983) Children of divorce: stress and developmental tasks. In Gamezy N, Rutter M (Eds) Stress, Coping and Development in Children. New York: McGraw-Hill.

Wallerstein JS, Kelly JB (1980) Surviving the Breakup: How Children and Parents Cope with Divorce. New York: Basic Books.

Weinberg WA, Rutman J, Sullivan L, Penick EC, Dietz SG (1973) Depression in children referred to an educational diagnostic center: diagnosis and treatment. Journal of Paediatrics 83: 1065–72.

Weissman MM, Klerman GL (1977) Sex differences and the epidemiology of depression. Archives of General Psychiatry 34: 98–111.

Weissman MM, Klerman GL (1978) Epidemiology of mental disorders. Archives of General Psychiatry 35: 705–12.

Weissman MM, Fendrich M, Warner V, Wickramaratne P (1992) Incidence of psychiatric disorder in offspring at high and low risk for depression. Journal of the American Academy of Child & Adolescent Psychiatry 31: 640–8.

Weissman MM, Gammon GD, John K, Merikangas KR, Warner V, Prusoff BA, Sholomsky D (1987) Children of depressed parents: increased psychopathology and early onset of major depression. Archives of General Psychiatry 44: 847–53.

Weissman MM, Gershon ES, Kidd KK, Prusoff BA, Leekman JF, Dibble E, Hamont J, Thompson WD, Pauls DL, Guroff JJ (1984a) Psychiatric disorders in the relatives of probands with affective disorders ... . Archives of General Psychiatry 41: 13–21.

Weissman MM, John K, Merikangas KR, Prusoff BA, Wickramaratne P, Gammon GD, Angold A, Warner V (1986) Depressed parents and their children: general health, social and psychiatric problems. American Journal of Diseases of Children 140: 801–5.

Weissman MM, Prusoff BA, Gammon GD, Merikangas KB, Leckmann JF, Kidd KK (1984b) Psychopathology in the children (ages 6–18) of depressed and normal parents. Journal of the American Academy of Child and Adolescent Psychiatry 23: 78–84.

Wetterburg L (1983) The relationship between the pineal gland and the pituitary adrenal axis in health, endocrine and psychiatric conditions. Psychoneuroendocrinology 8: 75–80.

Whitaker A, Johnson J, Shaffer D, Rapoport JL, Kalikow K, Walsh BT, Davies M, Braiman S, Dolinsky A (1990) Uncommon troubles in young people ... Archives of General Psychiatry 47, 487–96.

Winokur G. (1978) Mania and depression: family studies and genetics in relation to treatment. In Lipton MA, Di Mascio A, Killam KF (Eds) Psychopharmacology: a Generation of Progress. New York: Raven.

Yaylayan S, Weller EB, Weller RA (1992) Neurobiology of depression. In Shafii M, Shafii SL (Eds) Clinical Guide to Depression in Children and Adolescents. Washington DC: American Psychiatric Association.

Young W, Knowles JB, MacLean AW, Boag L, McConville BJ (1982) The sleep of childhood depressives: comparison with age matched controls. Biological Psychiatry 17: 1163–8.

Zeitlin M (1972) M.Phil thesis, University of London.

Chapter 2
Clinical Assessment and Planning for Treatment

INGRID DAVISON

Introduction

The concept of depression in children has evolved since the mid-1970s. It used to be thought that depression did not occur until adolescence or, if it did occur, that its symptoms were masked by other problems such as aggression or anxiety. This led to the unfortunate situation in which a number of differing presentations, including conduct disorder and school refusal, might be diagnosed as 'masked' depression by some psychiatrists whereas other psychiatrists maintained that childhood depression did not exist. Little attempt was made by either group to search for core symptoms of depression such as lowered mood.

This lack of clear thinking about depression may be partly attributable to the fact that the condition often coexists with other disorders such as conduct disorder or school refusal. Kolvin *et al.* (1991) found that 35% of children who were referred to the outpatient department of a university child psychiatry unit had significant depression but that this could be misdiagnosed unless children with other psychiatric diagnoses were examined closely. Children with so-called masked depressive disorders may well be overtly depressed but their depressive symptoms may not have been sought sufficiently rigorously. It is therefore important for clinicians to examine children for depression even when they present with other more obvious conditions.

It is now accepted that the essential features of depression are similar in children, adolescents and adults but there are some developmental differences. Children are less able than adults to describe their feelings accurately and they probably experience less sophisticated nuances of feeling. Guilt and hopelessness, for example, are concepts that children may find difficult to experience and articulate. Children generally tend to somatize their feelings more than adults, so physical symptoms may present more prominently. Finally, children and adults lead their lives in different situations and some symptoms of depression may be expressed in settings specific to children (for example, school performance may deteriorate).

The following list outlines the most common symptoms of depression in childhood:

Lowered mood that persists over time
Increased or reduced weight
Increased or reduced appetite
Persistent insomnia or hypersomnia
Loss of interest in usual activities
Withdrawal from social activity
Excessive tiredness
Irritability
Impaired concentration
Agitation or reduced level of activity
Deteriorating performance in school
Feelings of worthlessness
Thoughts of self-harm
Attempts at self-harm
Non-organic physical symptoms such as abdominal pain

Clinical assessment

Taking a full clinical, personal and family history from a family, examining a child's mental state, and obtaining other relevant information from a variety of sources are all basic skills in child psychiatry. They are of particular importance, however, in the assessment of depression. Barrett *et al.* (1991) found that there was considerable disagreement between parents and children in the reporting of depressive symptoms, with parents tending to underestimate the frequency of subjective symptoms such as self-dislike, a sense of failure and, most worryingly, suicidal ideas and attempts at self-harm. It is therefore vitally important to interview the child alone, but this is not to undervalue the interview with the parents and the rest of the family who often have valuable insights into the child's functioning of which the child in question may be unaware.

Interviewing the family

Cox (1994a) suggests that continued attendance at the clinic is more likely if individual contacts follow a family assessment than if a family meeting follows individual interviews with parents and the child. Family members can also provide observations and information which can be followed up later individually with the child. For these reasons, most clinicians begin their assessment with a meeting that includes as many family members living at home with the child as can attend.

There are as many different ways of conducting a clinical interview as there are clinical interviewers. It must be remembered, however, that the purpose of the clinical assessment in possible cases of depression is to elicit sufficient information to make a diagnosis and to gain enough of an understanding about the severity and context of the disorder to plan a treatment programme.

The interview begins with introductions and the reason for the meeting is clarified. This is important because communication in families may be poor and some family members may not know why they are present. Lies may sometimes have been told to children in order to persuade them to attend. This puts the clinician in an intolerable position and may infuriate the child if it is not exposed at the outset. Families are often put at ease at this stage if they are given some idea about how the interview will proceed and when it is likely to finish.

Cox (1994b) points out that systematic questioning is superior to free reporting for obtaining full and detailed information about a child's symptoms, but that parents spontaneously talk about the child's presenting problems and family background. Several studies have linked 'patient satisfaction' (Stewart, 1984) and 'compliance with medical recommendations' (Carter *et al.*, 1982) with an open listening approach by the interviewer which encourages the patient to tell his or her own story. In view of this, an invitation to the family to talk freely at the outset of the interview, followed by a specific enquiry about the child's symptoms and background would seem to be most appropriate. Questions should be open rather than closed in order to allow the family to provide as much detailed information as possible. Thus, for example, when asking a parent about a child's difficult behaviour it is better to ask 'how did you feel about that?' and 'what did you do about that?' rather than 'did that make you feel cross?' and 'did you punish him or her?'

The enquiry needs to be wide ranging. The interviewer is not only interested in listing symptoms of depression; symptoms of any other disorder which may coexist with it must also be noted. Depressed children often have multiple psychosocial problems which may have precipitated the depressive episode and which will certainly influence its course. Such problems may need tackling in their own right or may need to be taken into account when planning treatment.

The child's present functioning, including her or his progress in school and relationships with peers and family members, are of obvious importance, particularly in relation to the child's sense of self-esteem and value. An account of his or her developmental history and premorbid personality is important in assessing the degree of vulnerability exhibited by the child. Educational support or social skills training may be required alongside more specific treatment for depression. An assessment of parental psychopathology is essential. Harrington *et al.* (1993) found that the prevalence of depressive disorder in the relatives of depressed children was double that in relatives of closely matched, non-depressed controls, suggesting a genetic element in the etiology of childhood depression. Clinical impressions certainly suggest that, to obtain a satisfactory outcome if parental and childhood depression coexist in a family, it is important to treat both parent and child.

The link between life events and childhood depression has been extensively studied. Depressive symptoms have been linked with abuse and Famularo *et al.* (1992) estimate that 20% of maltreated children develop a depressive disorder. Goodyer *et al.* (1988), however, suggest that the relationship between stressful life events and the type of childhood emotional disorder experienced is non-specific, with children as likely to become anxious in response to a trauma as they are to become depressed. When planning treatment, however, it is important to be aware that a proportion of depressed children seem to be reacting to a specific life event, whether it be the death of a relative, bullying at school, or a traumatic sexual experience.

The initial family interview gives the clinician an opportunity to make a superficial assessment of family functioning. This is important, firstly because experience of a dysfunctional family may be contributing to the child's depression and, secondly, because planning treatment will depend on how much useful support the family is able to provide. Observations of the family's verbal and non-verbal interactions may give useful information about patterns of communication, allocation of roles, and the permeability of boundaries within the family from which initial tentative hypotheses regarding structure and functioning can be made. Of course, if family therapy seems to be an appropriate method of treatment, a more detailed assessment of the family may need to take place at a later date.

Interviewing the child

It is of the utmost importance to see the child alone in order to explore subjective symptoms of depression and to observe the child's behaviour. The interview should take place in a private, child-friendly setting where there are no anxieties about being overheard. It is often useful to begin by reminding the child of the purpose of the interview and giving her or him some idea of what will take place. The child may be set at ease if the initial questions relate to emotionally neutral areas of his or her life where she or he may be achieving some success, such as activities out of school. The interviewer should have some idea of where to start from the earlier interview with the family.

The general principles for interviewing children are similar to those for interviewing parents or families. The child should be invited to give his or her own account of events and this can be followed by specific enquiries using age-appropriate open questions. It may be appropriate to ask an adolescent about feelings of guilt but a younger child is unlikely to give a meaningful answer to such a question. It is often relevant to enquire about physical symptoms when assessing young children for depression but the clinician should refer to 'tummy ache' rather than 'abdominal pain'. Younger children should not be asked whether they have ever contemplated suicide but rather whether they have ever thought of hurting themselves.

Evaluation of the risk of suicide is obviously a vital part of the clinical assessment of depression. Children should be asked about the frequency and persistence of thoughts of self-harm, the method they might employ, and whether they have ever acted on their thoughts. If so, they should be asked whether the attempt was planned, whether they took precautions to ensure secrecy, whether they were discovered and whether they intended to kill themselves. Some indication of their view of themselves and their future should be sought because hopelessness and self-blame have been linked to suicidal intent (Beck *et al.*, 1985). Other problems, including conduct disorder and substance misuse, have been associated with an increased risk of self-harm and Shaffer and Piacentini (1994) suggest that the following risk factors should be considered especially seriously:

Male sex
Adolescents with persistent ideation or history of recurrent attempts at self-harm
Children who consider using a method other than ingestion or superficial cutting.
Children with significant psychiatric disorder or who indulge in substance abuse.
Children with no reliable family to ensure their safety.

Observation of the child

The interview with the child allows the clinician to observe his or her appearance and behaviour carefully. Is the child clean, and appropriately and adequately dressed, or are there signs of neglect? How do the child and the parents cope with separation? Is the level of separation anxiety appropriate to the age of the child? It may, in some cases, be impossible to interview the child without the presence of the parent. Alternatively, the child may separate too easily and by her or his indiscriminate over-friendly behaviour suggest a history of early emotional deprivation.

What is the child's approximate developmental level? Is it appropriate for his or her age? Developmental delay and physical or emotional immaturity are obvious disadvantages for a child. Some children, however, are unusually well grown and emotionally mature or gifted for their age. This may sometimes be a mixed blessing.

It is normal for children to appear wary and reticent at the start of an interview but most will settle down and relax given time. This allows observation of their social skills with an adult in a one-to-one setting. Does the child make good eye contact? Can he or she establish a rapport with the clinician? Is her or his behaviour socially appropriate? Can he or she maintain a conversation?

Observation of affect is particularly important in the assessment of depression. What is the child's facial expression? Does she or he smile appropriately? Is he or she tearful? Is there any evidence of excessive anxiety? Is she or he normally emotionally responsive? Is his or her posture appropriate?

Motor activity may be affected by depression. Is the child over-active and agitated? Is she or he underactive and slow? The presence of motor abnormalities such as tics or stereotypies should also be noted.

Is the form of the child's speech normal? Slow, stumbling speech may occur in depression but it is important to be aware of other abnormalities such as stuttering or verbal tics. Is the content of the child's speech appropriate? Is there any sign of thought disorder? Does the child have any unusual preoccupations or beliefs? Severe psychotic depression in childhood is rare but it does occur and may involve persecutory auditory hallucinations or delusions of guilt and self-blame.

Finally, a brief assessment of cognitive function, such as concentration and short-term memory, may be helpful.

Information from other sources

During term time children spend approximately one-third of their waking hours in school. This is a setting where they are expected to conform to established routines, to function as part of a group of peers, and to achieve goals within specified time limits. Information from the teacher about a child's functioning in school can therefore be invaluable in the assessment of the child's social adjustment and educational progress.

Information from school must, however, be considered in context. It is not unusual for a severely depressed child to assume a cheerful facade for the benefit of her or his teachers and peers and it is unrealistic to expect teachers to know a child as well as his or her parents. It must also be remembered that teachers tend to be more aware of the problems of disruptive, aggressive children than those of quiet withdrawn children.

Other sources of information include Scout and Guide leaders, youth club organizers, teachers of extra-curricular activities such as religious education, dancing, riding and so forth. The permission of the family must obviously be obtained before approaching any of these individuals.

Aids in diagnosis

A variety of tools for assessing depression have been developed as research interest in childhood depression has grown in recent years. Self-rating questionnaires to be completed by children themselves have been particularly popular and, of these, the Child Depression Inventory (Kovacs, 1981) is probably the most widely used (Kazdin, 1990). This includes 27 items relating to the signs and symptoms of depression. The child reads them and then, for each item, selects one of three alternative statements that is most applicable to her or him during the last two weeks. The Child Depression Inventory is well researched and has been shown to be internally consistent and reliable over time (Kazdin, 1990). It is particularly useful as a screening instrument.

A number of standardized interviews have also been developed. The Schedule for Affective Disorders and Schizophrenia (Kiddie-SADS) (Chambers *et al.*, 1985) is typical of these. It begins with a general enquiry about the child's symptoms and adjustment followed by a large number of specific questions about a wide range of symptoms across a number of psychiatric disorders. Parent and child are interviewed separately. Several studies have shown that this, and similar standardized interviews, generate reliable and valid diagnoses of depression and this has greatly facilitated research into childhood depression (Kazdin, 1990).

There has been great interest in developing psychobiological markers of depression and, in adults, the Dexamethasone Suppression Test has been used to distinguish patients with endogenous depression from those with reactive depression (Dam, 1985). This test involves administering dexamethasone, a synthetic corticosteroid, and measuring the level of the cortisol secretions over the next 24 hours. Cortisol secretion is suppressed in normal subjects but is relatively high in those with endogenous depression. Unfortunately, the Dexamethasone Suppression Test has not been shown to be helpful in distinguishing between depressed and non-depressed cases in children (Tyrer *et al.*, 1991) and clinicians do not consider it to be a useful tool in the assessment of childhood depression.

Formulating a diagnosis

Thorough clinical assessment yields a large volume of information which must be organized and interpreted before making a definitive diagnosis and planning a treatment programme.

Consideration needs to be given to the developmental context of signs and symptoms. Behaviour that might cause great concern in an adult, or even in an adolescent, may be developmentally normal in a younger child. Weekly temper outbursts in a toddler are to be expected but they are a significant problem in an adolescent. When children enter education at the age of five, tears often occur every morning for a short period, but this behaviour would be much more worrying in a 12 year old.

Information regarding frequency, persistence and pervasiveness of subjective depressive symptoms and their impact on functioning is of vital importance in determining the severity of depression. Obviously, a symptom such as tearfulness, which has occurred daily for several months at home and at school and when out playing, and which has resulted in the child being sent home early from a camping trip, is much more significant than a single episode of tears following an argument with a friend.

Once a diagnosis of depression has been made it needs to be understood in the context of any other problems with which the child is presenting and against the background of his or her personal and family history. The diagnosis of depression may be common but it will not have exactly the same significance for any two sufferers. The planning of treatment will involve different issues in different cases. Clinical examples help to illustrate this point.

'X' was a 16-year-old girl of above-average intelligence who presented with a 3-month history of lowered mood, irritability, insomnia and impaired appetite. She felt constantly tired and unable to concentrate. She had suicidal thoughts and, indeed, took an overdose shortly after referral. Surprisingly, her school work remained excellent as did her social relationships although her teachers noticed that she was quieter with her friends than usual. Her symptoms of depression were apparently precipitated by her disclosure of sexual abuse within her family – a disclosure that her parents and other family members declined to believe.

'Y' was an 11-year-old boy who had long-standing minor learning difficulties in school. He was referred with an 18-month history of behavioural and social difficulties in school since transferring from primary to secondary education. On enquiry it transpired that this move had coincided with a very acrimonious breakdown in his parents' marriage, following which both had found new partners. 'Y' exhibited intense sadness, tearfulness, irritability, insomnia, social withdrawal and impaired concentration. His performance in school deteriorated and he lacked motivation to complete homework assignments. He felt worthless and guilty and had thought of harming himself.

Planning for treatment

Case management

A distinction should be made between management strategies and specific therapies in the treatment of depression. Case management involves decisions about the setting and goals of treatment whereas therapy involves the use of particular forms of treatment designed to tackle particular problems.

Perhaps the most important initial management decision relates to the setting of the treatment. Should the child be admitted to hospital or can he or she be treated as an outpatient? With children it is obviously important to avoid inpatient admission and separation from the family if possible. In the vast majority of cases outpatient treatment will be perfectly adequate. In cases of severe depression, however, particularly if there is a serious risk of self-harm, or if the family is unable to provide the necessary support at home, admission may be required. A period of day-patient treatment may be helpful for youngsters with less severe symptoms and appropriate family support but who may still require intense treatment or relief from the daily demands of the school routine. For most children, however, outpatient treatment will be the most appropriate choice.

Management decisions about the goals of treatment will also need to be made at this initial stage. This will, of course, depend on the range of problems identified during assessment. In the case of 'X' above, it was decided that individual therapy should take place with 'X' herself to tackle the issue of sexual abuse, and that family therapy was also necessary to help her parents in particular to respond more appropriately to her. Finally, specific treatment of 'X's depression was required. In the case of 'Y', educational support in school was offered together with social skills training and work with the parents to help them manage their conflict more appropriately, alongside specific treatment of 'Y's depression. This raises issues concerning the timing and pacing of treatment because it can be unhelpful to overwhelm children and their families with simultaneous treatment options. It may be helpful to postpone intensive individual psychotherapy or family therapy until the child has started to recover from the depression and is better able to use this help.

In some mild cases, where the child's depression is an understandable reaction to an event, the family is understanding, and functioning is not seriously impaired, a low-key approach offering occasional discussions and monitoring and encouraging the family to support the child may be sufficient (Harrington, 1992).

Specific antidepressant therapies

Research into the treatment of childhood depression is at a relatively early stage when compared with the knowledge we have about the treatment of depression in adults. Most studies of treatment have examined therapies which are known to be effective with adults because the general consensus is that adult and childhood depression are essentially similar (Harrington, 1992).

Studies of the efficacy of antidepressant drugs, particularly tricyclic antidepressants, have been disappointing in children. For example, Geller *et al.* (1992) found no significant difference in the rate of response between Nortriptyline and a placebo, even though his subjects, 6–12 year olds with diagnosed depression, had already undergone a two-week trial with a placebo and those children who had responded to the placebo at this stage were excluded. Tricyclic antidepressants are known to be effective in adults and the reason for this discrepancy in children is unclear. Harrington (1992) suggests that depressed young people may be a heterogeneous group and studies so far may have included children who are resistant to antidepressants. Alternatively, early onset depression may be more severe than adult depression and therefore more resistant to drugs, or there may be some difference in brain neurochemistry between children and adults that prevents antidepressants from acting. This lack of clarity means that antidepressant drugs are not seen as a first-line treatment in childhood depression and they tend to be used only with those youngsters presenting with severe depression.

Research into specific psychological therapies has been similarly limited in extent but it has produced more promising results. Cognitive behavioural therapy seems to be particularly effective. For example, Lewinsohn *et al.* (1990) found that a cognitive behavioural group intervention, including cognitive therapy, relaxation and social skills training, produced significant improvement in depressed adolescents, and Stark (1990) found that cognitive therapy was more effective than non-directive counselling in the treatment of depressed adolescents. Many therapists also advocate individual psychotherapy or family therapy because, empirically, it seems to make sense to involve young people and their parents in discussions about the nature and course of the depression and in tackling solutions to the problems that have probably contributed to it. It must be remembered, however, that research into such interventions is still at a very early stage and there is, as yet, very little evidence that individual psychotherapy or family therapy are specifically effective treatments for depression.

As in all child psychiatry, choice of treatment will depend upon the nature of the depression and its associated problems, the agreement and involvement of the young person and his or her family, and the skills and inclination of the therapist. Most child psychiatrists adopt an eclectic approach and use a combination of interventions.

References

Barrett ML, Berney TP, Bhate SR, Famuyiwa OO, Fundudis T, Kolvin I, Tyrer S (1991) Diagnosing childhood depression: who should be interviewed – parent or child? The Newcastle Child Depression Project. British Journal of Psychiatry 159: (suppl. 11) 22–7.

Beck AT, Steer RA, Kovacs M, Garrison B (1985) Hopelessness and eventual suicide: a 10-year prospective study of patients hospitalized with suicidal ideation. American Journal of Psychiatry 142: 559–62.

Carter WB, Inui TS, Kukull W, Haigh V (1982) Outcome-based doctor–patient interaction analysis II: identifying effective provider and patient behaviour. Medical Care 20: 550–66.

Chamber WJ, Puig-Antich J, Hirsch M, Paez P, Ambrosini PJ, Tabrizi MA, Davies M (1985) The assessment of affective disorders in children and adolescents by semistructured interview: test–retest reliability. Archives of General Psychiatry 42: 696–702.

Cox A (1994a) Diagnostic appraisal. In Rutter M, Taylor E, Hersov L (Eds) Child and Adolescent Psychiatry: Modern Approaches. Oxford: Blackwell Scientific Publications.

Cox A (1994b) Interviews with parents. In Rutter M, Taylor E, Hersov L (Eds) Child and Adolescent Psychiatry: Modern Approaches. Oxford: Blackwell Scientific Publications.

Dam H, Mellerup ET, Rafaelson OJ (1985) The dexamethasone suppression test in depression. Journal of Affective Disorders 8: 95–103.

Famularo R, Kinscherff R, Fenton T (1992) Psychiatric diagnoses of maltreated children: preliminary findings. Journal of the American Academy of Child and Adolescent Psychiatry 31: 863–7.

Geller B, Cooper TB, Graham DL, Fetner HH, Marsteller FA, Wells JM (1992) Pharmaco-kinetically designed double-blind placebo controlled study of Nortriptyline in 6–12 year olds with major depressive disorder. Journal of the American Academy of Child and Adolescent Psychiatry 31: 34–44.

Goodyer IM, Wright C, Altham PME (1988) Maternal adversity and recent stressful life events in anxious and depressed children. Journal of Child Psychology and Psychiatry 29: 651–67.

Harrington R (1992) The natural history and treatment of child and adolescent affective disorders. British Journal of Child Psychology and Psychiatry 33: 1287–302.

Harrington RC, Fudge H, Rutter M, Bredenkamp D, Groothues C, Pridham J (1993) Child and adult depression: a test of continuities with data from a family study. British Journal of Psychiatry 162: 627–33.

Kazdin AE (1990) Childhood depression. Journal of Child Psychology and Psychiatry 31: 121–60.

Kolvin I, Barrett ML, Bhate SR, Berney TP, Famuyiwa OO, Fundudis T, Tyrer S (1991) The Newcastle Child Depression Project: diagnosis and classification of depression. British Journal of Psychiatry 159 (suppl. 11) 9–21.

Kovacs M (1981) Rating scales to assess depression in school-aged children. Acta Paedopsychiatrica 46: 305–15.

Lewinsohn PM, Clarke GN, Hops H, Andrews SJ (1990) Cognitive-behavioural treatment for depressed adolescents. Behaviour Therapy 21: 385–401.

Shaffer D, Piacentini J (1994) Suicide and attempted suicide. In Rutter M, Taylor E, Hersov L (Eds) Child and Adolescent Psychiatry: Modern Approaches. Oxford: Blackwell Scientific Publications.

Stark KD (1990) Childhood Depression: School-based Intervention. New York: Guilford.

Stewart M (1984) What is a successful doctor–patient interview? A study of interactions and outcomes. Social Science and Medicine 19: 167–75.

Tyrer SP, Barrett ML, Berney TP, Bhate S, Watson MJ, Fundudis T, Kolvin I (1991) The Dexamethasone Suppression Test in children: lack of an association with diagnosis. The Newcastle Child Depression Project. British Journal of Psychiatry 159 (suppl. 11) 41–8.

Chapter 3
The Family Background:
the Social Worker's Input

JOAN HUTTEN

The societal context of depression

Social workers in an interdisciplinary mental health team are, by definition, the people who keep in mind the social and the societal dimensions of disorders. This need not mean that other team members are blind to such factors, nor that they ignore intra-psychic processes or genetic differences. What, then, are the current social realities that influence the manifestation of depression in children and young people?

We live in a time of worldwide political, religious and economic upheaval which is manifested as war, terrorism, repression, starvation, poverty and deviance. All of these may lead to migration and the experience of conflicting social mores. If we add the changes in family size and values, more common divorce and remarriage, mobile work patterns and the demographic changes from greatly increased life expectancy in the developed world, the ability of the family and community to perform protective functions for young and old is vastly eroded. Feminism has affected the way we think about half the population in relation to career satisfaction and opportunity. The shedding of the taboos on sexual abuse and exploitation together with the new risk of AIDS have sharpened individual responsibility. At the same time the emergence of highly competitive employment practices, and the advent of distance communication by computer, fax and telephone have rudely altered traditional patterns of interdependence so that children, like adults, inhabit a world that fosters depression.

Traditional understandings of the *meaning* of work and social roles no longer apply. There has probably always been widespread ambivalence about the relative priority to be given to the needs of children and the needs of adults but this is currently exacerbated by legitimately short-term business planning (because technological change makes longer-term planning unrealistic) and by managerial styles which favour quick solutions (and profits) regardless of long-term consequences. There can rarely have been such a poor fit between educational opportunity, caring needs and employment prospects. Who cares about the future?

Writers are often intuitively aware of social trends ahead of theoreticians. Reading Dickens or Mark Twain gives one an historical perspective on the social realities for children. More recently there has been a spate of novels and films about the enormous changes in lifestyle within one or two generations in the Australian outback, the American midwest, Africa, India and the Far East. We need to know what facilitates the transitions which children are expected to make within one lifetime. Parents may be ill-placed geographically or intellectually to transmit appropriate wisdom. Inner city anomie and isolating computer addiction offer no succour in moments of existential anguish.

Pathological religious sects have sprung up to offer sometimes disastrous panaceas to the perplexed and alienated young. The society section of the *Guardian* recently devoted a leading article to the treatment of troubled young minds, deploring the 50% increase in hospitalization of children under 10 with mental health problems in the years 1991–2. Child guidance services have been cut back or obliterated in the name of rationalization and adults have so little time for children that, faced with increasingly insistent messages from them, they can only resort to expensive and ineffective institutional 'remedies' which temporarily remove the problem but ultimately make things worse.

Supporting families in stress

Social workers, like other professionals, are caught in this speeded-up world and have to rethink the strategies they employ to intervene helpfully. Past experience suggests that troublesome children attract much more attention, helpful or otherwise, than quietly depressed or withdrawn children receive. Parents often have problems of their own which militate against their being able to recognize the plight of children who fail to protest. Migrating parents may well have to send unaccompanied adolescents on ahead or leave their younger children with relatives until they have established a toehold in the new environment. Financially comfortable parents struggling with marital problems may well send their children to boarding school with the kindest of intentions but they cannot allow themselves to observe or hear the distress the children feel.

A case example discussed

As it is now some years since I was engaged in clinical work, I have had to draw on a case first described in my book *Short-term Contracts in Social Work*, published by Routledge and Kegan Paul in 1977. I hope it will be representative of cases one might encounter today and that it will indicate some of the contextual concerns I have outlined above.

Jeremy Anderson, aged 11 years 4 months, was the eldest son of Mr Anderson, aged 55 and Mrs Anderson, aged 38. He had two brothers aged 10 and 9. At the beginning of the Spring term Jeremy was referred to the clinic by his Head Teacher who thought him to be 'on the verge of a nervous breakdown'. The referral was supported by the family doctor. The initial assessment interview with the mother and father revealed a behaviour change dating back four months, following a bout of 'flu and his maternal grandmother's unexpected death. Jeremy had suddenly become weepy and withdrawn and, at school, solitary and antisocial. Both parents were irritated and distressed by the school's referral and did not agree with the school's assessment of Jeremy's mental state. Although the Andersons felt angry and defensive, they showed concern for their son's reported difficulties. They thought he might be reacting to a series of events and agreed to continue meeting, together with Jeremy, to explore his problems with the team, composed of a social worker and a psychologist.

The first appointment offered was attended late and only by Mr Anderson and Jeremy. Mrs Anderson was attending a meeting concerned with rehousing. The family was inadequately housed in two rooms, all family members shared the same bedroom. The father considered *this* to be the basis of Jeremy's difficulties and nothing to do with the school, the area we had suggested we might explore. Mr Anderson announced that he had no time for such nonsense, asked his son to come along and left saying that his wife would contact us as Jeremy thought he might like to return to the clinic. She did this and we subsequently offered a series of five weekly appointments, all of which were cancelled indirectly at the last minute, yet always with a request for another one.

To determine our strategy and how we might be of help to the Andersons, we contacted the relevant network: the school, the doctor and the social services department.

The school reported that Jeremy was so troublesome, fighting, leaving class and truanting, that he was in danger of suspension. The doctor spoke highly of the Anderson boys and Mr Anderson and admitted that although he had attended all boys since birth and treated Mr Anderson for angina, he had never seen Mrs Anderson. He believed the Andersons to have a stable cohabitee relationship and to be the natural parents of the boys – yet he knew the Anderson name to be an alias, that Mr Anderson had a hidden past and had been charged with exhibitionism. The social services department were currently involved in the rehousing issue, with the doctor's support, but found the Andersons to be standoffish and defensive, wanting no help whatsoever.

One month after the first dramatic meeting with Jeremy and his father, Jeremy and his mother arrived for their appointment late. The school had in the meantime suspended Jeremy, yet both mother and son insisted it was by mutual agreement and because of a misunderstanding.

Jeremy, throughout the session, appeared depressed and spoke of his feelings of hopelessness and despair. He stuttered badly and bit his fingernails. He longed for more space and a new school, yet felt it was all in vain. He agreed to come back only if his brothers did not know and did not come.

Both mother and son thought an appropriate focus would be on Jeremy's school difficulties and agreed to a contract for eight weekly meetings, to include Mr Anderson over the next two months and to have Jeremy take psychological tests for the purpose of deciding on the best school placement for him as he was in his final year in primary school. The mother felt the housing was none of our concern and refused any offer of help. Mrs Anderson and Jeremy kept all arranged appointments. They arrived twenty minutes late, never together and never with Mr Anderson. Apologies and excuses were always given for his absence and their lateness and the subject dropped. As Jeremy and the psychologist worked on the test material, Mrs Anderson and the social worker met together. Mrs Anderson remained defensive and lighthearted, seeing improvement and underestimating any problems of hers, the family's or Jeremy's.

For the session in which the results of tests were reported back, the father joined Jeremy and his mother. Jeremy was found to be of high-average intelligence, but underachieving and having emotional difficulties. His behaviour during the testing was reluctant, resistant and obsessive. The recommendation made was for placement in a boarding school for maladjusted children which the parents and Jeremy reacted violently against and flatly refused to accept. They requested a further series of meetings to explore and work out a more suitable school alternative. We renegotiated a second contract for six more weekly meetings until the summer break. Both parents and Jeremy attended these. The father very much took the role of leader and focuser throughout this second series, with mother and Jeremy understating any problems. The school placement was dealt with immediately by Jeremy being accepted by a comprehensive school of the Andersons' choice. The next area focused on by the father was Jeremy's emotional problems ...

Mr Anderson then brought up the problem of the father/son relationship and Jeremy's lack of confidence in himself and his preference always to be with his father. Both parents felt they expected Jeremy to act much older than his years and maybe were robbing him of his youth, thereby contributing to the fights among the brothers.

A family pattern was identified of the parents speaking for Jeremy and never listening to what he had to say. Jeremy's stutter became less evident as the sessions went on and in the penultimate session he shared his secret worries to do with the supernatural and how he always felt his parents wanted to be rid of him until they took the firm stand they did in refusing to allow him to be sent away to school. By the end of the second contract, the Andersons reviewed the improvement in Jeremy and in their family functioning in general. They had all decided to listen to each other. The school was finding Jeremy settled and happy again and the family had received confirmation that they would be rehoused. The two younger brothers were still considered a problem as far as the school was concerned, but not by the parents.

The Andersons found termination difficult, evidence that they had found the clinic experience to be a positive one in the end. They knew they were welcome to return at any time for whatever reason and that recontacting the clinic was their responsibility.

Nine months after their first contact, Mrs Anderson approached the clinic for help with Jeremy who was school refusing in his secondary school. An appointment was offered to the parents and Jeremy but only mother and son attended. Mrs Anderson stated clearly her desire for Jeremy to come for treatment for himself. Jeremy refused, saying he would prefer to go back to school if only he could be excused from physical education and drama. The problem was felt to be between the Andersons and the school. Mrs Anderson offered to explore this with the education welfare officer and be back in touch.

Although nothing more was heard directly from the Andersons, soon the education welfare officer phoned asking for reports and help for the school in dealing with the recurrent school crisis. Based on her previous experience of the Andersons' ability to cope with problems on their own if given encouragement and the knowledge of Jeremy's recent refusal of help for himself, the clinic social worker suggested a meeting at school which might include herself, the Andersons and all the school staff concerned. She offered to inform the Andersons of the school's concern and request for help and to invite them to the meeting. The school agreed in principle to the meeting but queried the wisdom of the parents and child being included. The compromise reached was that only the parents would be invited. The school was aware that the Andersons had ended their contact with the clinic a year ago and were reluctant to become involved again. It accepted the challenge of the problem with Jeremy being now their problem and, with the clinic's support, was prepared to become engaged with the parents in attempting to work out a mutually acceptable solution.

The clinic social worker felt her role in the school meeting to be that of enabler and anticipated using herself and her interventions in a limited and focused way so that both the school and the parents might address themselves to the task in hand and resolve their problems.

The school meeting lasted an hour and went through three distinct phases. The first phase involved both school and parents taking up defensive positions, each feeling it was the other's fault (and each blaming the other). The second phase was more task-orientated with the school taking the lead and sharing with the parents their genuine interest in Jeremy as pupil and their wish to know how best to help him.

The third phase was a mutual engagement of the parents and school together in attempting to find solutions and resolutions to Jeremy's present and expressed school difficulties. The clinic social worker's conscious and planned use of herself through her appropriately placed comments and questions enabled the parties concerned to reach amicable, workable and acceptable solutions to the problems at hand. The result was that the school and the parents felt a relieved sense of achievement. The parents acknowledged the help given them by saying they no longer felt there was a need for Jeremy to return to the clinic. The school on the other hand asked if more help could be given to them by the clinic in the future, for they had many difficulties with other children. At this moment the school felt both pride and satisfaction that they had dealt successfully with one very difficult and persistent problem.

We can see from the above case something of the complexity of diagnosis and intervention. Here is a pubertal boy who has recently been exposed to a death in the family and his own experience of illness. Surrounding him are loving parents who nevertheless have secrets, and younger siblings for whom he is made to feel responsible. Their immediate environment is grossly inadequate housing, where all the family sleep in the same room. In the wider environment we learn that the school finds the boy solitary and antisocial, and on the verge of a nervous breakdown.

The professional team that encounters these phenomena clearly has to recognize the limits of its power. It is not omnipotent. The family are not immediately compliant and grateful. Dealing only with intra-psychic factors will not solve the problem. There is unlikely to be any 'ideal' solution. Similarly, professional curiosity about how the father's secret past impinges on the family has to be curbed in the interests of working in the 'here and now' with limited resources. The wider social ramifications are largely outside the team's remit but are undoubtedly significant.

The first task has to be to convert a referral into a therapeutic alliance. The father reacts with suspicion and impatience, the mother and son cancel their appointments and persistently deny the importance of the problem, hoping it will just go away. The team eventually engages the trio by thinking about its experience of this family, listening to what its members say, and taking it seriously, reflecting back the evidence. Magic transformations are not expected but somehow the experience of receiving attention enables the family to engage with the housing and educational bureaucracies with a little hope rather than a self-fulfilling expectation of frustration and disappointment. Something happens inside Jeremy too. From being withdrawn and weepy he is now described as 'troublesome, fighting and truanting'. He stutters less. One might say that the rage that had been turned inward in depression was now beginning to be turned outward – that he, too, was searching with a glimmer of hope. This evokes more urgent action by the school and he is suspended and in the subsequent clinic interview he easily swings back to his earlier 'hopelessness and despair', but this time he is able to acknowledge his feelings and confide some of his anxieties, with rudimentary hope. There is no dramatic 'happy-ever-after' solution but what has been learned from experience is not unlearned and when a later crisis occurs, the family takes the initiative in seeking support for further engagement with their environment and the clinic staff enable them to do just that without needing to be involved as central figures themselves. Authority derives from the task, not from the roles or ideologies and institutions involved.

Society and the professionals

Professionals have always been at risk of subtly promoting their own status and interests notwithstanding their genuinely altruistic endeavours. When the end of 'the dependency culture' becomes politically correct, a great effort has to be made to develop leadership into therapeutic alliances and self-help. It is so tempting to blame the political, economic and managerial climate for one's failure to shift the balance from deterioration to improvement. All too often a verbal or pharmaceutical prescription is handed out without time for subsequent reassessment or dialogue, with the result that inadequate and even harmful strategies are perpetuated without responsible follow-up. Maybe one of the positive by-products of today's situation is that the professionals themselves are more aware of the system impinging on themselves and of what helps and what does not help. When we ourselves are suffering as a result of a lack of resources we can perhaps more easily understand those who are also experiencing the problem of how best to use the resources available and to preserve some autonomy and choice.

Stress can be simply defined as an absence of choice. Social workers have been caught up in that experience and there is a lot of evidence that, despite the removal of casework from the curriculum of social work training, surprisingly large numbers of qualified workers are paying their own fees for post-qualifying training in counselling or psychotherapy. They are at least in touch with their own needs and aware of what they themselves have found helpful.

Although there is decreasing scope or support for sustained relationship work in social services departments, there has been an expansion of voluntary sector services offering counselling to deal with primary school children, troubled marriages, AIDS sufferers, drug addicts, the dying and bereaved, victims of disasters, general practice patients, redundant employees, and the suicidal. It is recognized that time to articulate feelings and choices with a human sounding-board contributes to individual and social well-being.

I have recently had the privilege of supervising trainee counsellors on placement in an innovative service in inner-city, multi-ethnic primary schools. Children can be referred, or can refer themselves, for one hour a week of individual attention on school premises and can take advantage of other remedial or group facilities already operating. The hypothesis being closely monitored and researched is that the early recognition of problems and early intervention will be a sound investment both psychically and economically. Counselling trainees volunteer their time and are closely supervised by paid professionals. The 'Place to Be' or 'P2B' scheme has had generous publicity and school staff, children, and parents have acclaimed the results to date.

This is a very imaginative harnessing of training and service needs but it is certainly no nostrum to be implemented without skilled professional support. I have been struck yet again by how hard it is for even well-meaning and well-motivated adults to allow themselves to observe and attend to children's communication. It is easy to be censorious of parents who seem oblivious to their children's messages but we have probably all been at the receiving end of 'parents know best' – and that, in turn, makes it very difficult for us to engage respectfully with children. The child who is latent in all of us is re-evoked when we communicate with children and, with that, the pain and confusion of failed childhood communications. We can allow ourselves to recognize symbolism in a stage production or a novel but we tend to deny the symbolism of a child's play and drawings. This approach can be enriching and empowering, although it may force us to carry out some uncomfortable self-analysis. A child who is distressed about family disruption or violence is unable to attend to class work but the teacher struggling with over-large classes has neither the time nor the opportunity to attend to this. The child becomes a nuisance or a 'dreamer' and underachievement continues in a vicious spiral. When the child is able to experience attention and his or her anxiety or sadness can be articulated and considered, difficult situations can become detoxified and coping mechanisms released.

As a society we find it easier to devise after-school play schemes which fit in with parental work problems than to acknowledge children's need for a place to be themselves and to be observed and heard rather than entertained or instructed. I suspect that, until we can comfortably be in touch with our own angry or deprived or sad child-selves, we will continue to succumb to the temptation to let problems escalate until heroic and costly remedies are unavoidable.

Self-help groups have sprung up in ever-increasing numbers to support individuals with a wide range of problems. Sometimes these have been initiated by the individuals concerned, frustrated at the lack or poor quality of public care, and sometimes the stimulus has come from professionals who have been able to mobilize autonomous, self-interested groups. The Natural Childbirth Trust, the Samaritans, Gingerbread, the Playgroup movement, numerous disability groups and contact groups for individuals with rare conditions would be examples. New Pin, a mutual support group for depressed single parents, was started with some professional support but has become self-perpetuating and must have prevented many children being taken into care and many parents from losing confidence completely, abandoning their children, or committing suicide.

The value of bearing pain and impotence

This theme of the afflicted becoming the best healers is of particular relevance to the containment of depression. If you have never suffered from depression it is hard to acknowledge what courage and staying power are required to bear with it. While I was thinking about this chapter, I had the privilege of a conversation with a retired colleague who has borne recurrent bouts of 'familial' depression throughout her life. Her mother committed suicide when my informant was only eight; she herself was a political refugee but, before that was an issue, she was aware as a young child of being overwhelmed by feelings of sadness every few months. She later became aware that other members of her extended family also suffered in this way. Her education was disturbed and she was obliged to move to England where she managed to support herself and obtain training despite her handicap. Progressively working to fund herself through a number of professional trainings, she eventually became a social worker, a university teacher, a child therapist and an analyst. A distinguished career one would say but one marked by two suicide attempts, periods on medication, much psychoanalysis and periods of depression lasting six to eight weeks once or twice a year. It is peculiarly hard to accept that we as carers cannot always 'cure'. Sometimes we can only enable pain to be borne – but with such worthwhile results!

Depression is very irritating to the family members and colleagues who have to witness it and who experience the frustration of not being able to take it away. They are faced with having to bear it repeatedly and to cope with their own rage and disappointment. Fortunately, not all depression is of the kind that gives rise to such problems. The old categories of reactive and endogenous depression are no longer simple and clear-cut; life-events or physical illness can trigger both sorts. Manic-depressive swings can be observed in mourning and in reactions to trauma among those who have never been psychiatrically diagnosed, whereas those who have been so diagnosed may undergo crises or suffer from the side-effects of other medication. Social workers may be able to help families to bear with and think about their children's illness but I suspect that the experience of someone who non-judgementally bears with the guilt or frustration in other family members is more potent than any intellectual insight.

In recent years, family therapists have drawn on systems theory in their work with families. This has enabled generational patterns to be explored both in relation to possible genetic tendencies and in relation to experiences that have not been worked through and which continue to impinge on those who were not even born at the time of the traumatic events. The metabolism of awful events like murders or of secrets that have been held for too long requires patient containment and listening while they are articulated from each family member's perspective, allowing that there is no definitive version. Children have remarkable resilience if they are allowed to face reality honestly – a reality of which they may well be aware at some level even though they may 'not be allowed' to know it; similarly, families have an all-too-easy option of allowing their inarticulate children to suffer for conflicts which the adults are unwilling to face. That this is not necessarily a conscious process in no way lessens the problem for them all.

The professional challenge

Child guidance services are thin on the ground and under-staffed and suffer from divisive management: the health service, the school psychological service and the social services departments are all bent on developing their own empires. On the one hand liberating models of interdisciplinary collaboration and interchangeable roles have been developed but, on the other, services have been closed down or restricted because of interprofessional rivalry. We need to know which factors promote innovation and creativity and which promote cynicism and destruction.

Clearly, in times of change, it is not enough to stick rigidly to a job description devised for earlier conditions. One student whom I taught on a post-qualifying course was the nearly full-time social worker in a county child guidance service where the psychiatrist had only one working session a week and the psychologist only three. It fell to her, therefore, to do a lot of peripatetic preliminary sifting. She was an imaginative and creative woman and so she mobilized mutual help, volunteer help and a wide variety of network support, and had to take decisions which would earlier have had to be confirmed by one or both of the other two disciplines. The county authorities realized that they were benefiting from this cheap skilled input but there was no way they could see their way clear to providing an appropriate level of remuneration. No doubt the professional managers were congratulating themselves on their efficient budgeting, but in the end the woman in question moved to a better paid but less professionally and clinically challenging post. There are limits to the extent to which social workers and volunteers have to display altruism on behalf of the whole of society.

Looking to the future

We are indebted to Melanie Klein for recognizing and articulating the fact that the capacity to feel depression is a centrally important stage in human development. The tiny infant rages and feels persecuted when the mother is not available on demand to feed it. Later, if the mother is mature enough to bear this and reassure the infant that its rage has not destroyed her, the baby will ultimately realize that the absent, frustrating mother and the present, gratifying mother are one and the same person and will feel sad about the attacks and wish to repair the ravages. This process of feeling sad about one's actions and wishing to repair the damage caused by them will subsequently fluctuate throughout life and is of immense significance for the resolution of future difficulties in individual, group, and community relations. Religious intolerance, racial prejudice and nationalist politics are all versions of the process of projecting blame outside ourselves. Only when we can see that good and bad feelings are part of the human condition, that loving and hating impulses exist in us all, can we begin to address reality creatively and cooperatively, accepting and managing our conflicting feelings so that we can engage in valid reparative work.

Depression therefore extends over a long range, from an appropriate impulse to reparation via situationally induced feelings of helpless anxiety or suppressed anger, to a genetically influenced, life-threatening and intractable illness. How the individual concerned manages it will depend heavily on the quality of understanding experienced. If we, as parents, friends, colleagues and professionals, can bear to let ourselves recognize it, tolerate it and talk about it, the suffering individual, child or adult, is more likely to be able to live through it too and be able to resist the temptation to commit intentional or accidental suicide. Our society needs reparative impulses.

References

Cox AD, Pound A, Mills M, Puckering C, Owen AL (1991) Evaluation of a home-visiting and befriending scheme for young mothers. Journal of the Royal Society of Medicine 84: 217–20.

Hutten JM (1977) Short-term Contracts in Social Work. London: Routledge and Kegan Paul.

Klein M, Riviere J (1937) Love, Hate and Reparation: Two Lectures. London: Hogarth Press and Institute of Psychoanalysis.

Klein M (1950) Mourning and its relation to the manic depressive states. In Contributions to Psychoanalysis 1921–45. London: Hogarth.

Klein M (1963) Our Adult Worlds and Other Essays. London: Heinemann.

Lawrence WG (1982) Physical and Psychological Stress at Work. Dublin: European Foundation for the Improvement of Living and Working Conditions.

Marris P (1958) Widows and their Families. London: Routledge and Kegan Paul.

Marris P (1974) Loss and Change. London: Routledge and Kegan Paul.

Pound A. (1991) Management of child abuse in a voluntary agency (New Pin). Child Abuse Review 5: 7–10.

Pound A (1990) The development of attachment in adult life: the New Pin experiment. British Journal of Psychotherapy 7: 77–85.

Rickford F (1985) The treatment of troubled young minds. Guardian 8 March 1995.

Walker J. (1995) The Cost of Communication Breakdown. Newcastle: Relate Centre for Family Studies, University of Newcastle.

Winnicott DW (1958) Collected Papers: Through Paediatrics to Psycho-analysis. London: Tavistock.

Winnicott, DW (1965) The Maturational Processes and the Facilitating Environment. London: Hogarth.

Chapter 4
Psychodynamic Psychotherapy

BIDDY YOUELL

Young children sometimes have to work very hard to draw attention to their depression and to make adults recognize it for what it is. They depend on adults to see and understand what is going on and there is a natural reluctance in adults to do so. We, as a society, cling to an idea of childhood as a happy time: a sort of Wonderland where children wander safe, innocent and carefree. We have become used to recognizing, reluctantly, that children may sometimes be sad, frightened, confused, worried ... but depressed? That still seems to be going too far. By contrast, we are very willing to see depression as an unwanted but very common part of adult life. We share a common language about it: we speak freely of feeling 'depressed', 'low','empty', 'down' and even of 'hopelessness' and 'despair'.

Here are two extracts from referral letters received by a child and family outpatient clinic.

1. I would be grateful if you would see this difficult nine year old and his family. His parents have again asked for professional help with his behaviour. He is causing problems in the classroom by distracting other children and bringing sharp and dangerous instruments into the school from home. On other occasions he is aggressive and will do such things as bite into ink cartridges, causing mess all over himself and his things.

    His parents say that he seems bored much of the time and can show remorse after an episode of bad behaviour but he does not mend his ways. In spite of his parents' calm, reasoned approach, nightly homework is a source of constant friction. They are successful, intelligent people but feel they have run out of ideas as to how to control him and are willing to return to you for further guidance.

2. Please could you see this young lady (16) as a matter of some urgency. She is very depressed for reasons which she does not know. She has sought counselling but is not sure if it is helping her.

These two very typical referral letters, from the same general practitioner's practice, would seem to have little in common. On the one hand, exasperated parents are seeking help in the management of their difficult child and, on the other, an articulate adolescent is telling her doctor that she is depressed and wants help. Both referrals are correctly sent to the local multidisciplinary child mental health team. Both are taken seriously and discussed and allocated in a thorough and thoughtful way.

After two appointments, the adolescent girl decided to terminate the contact and enter fully into what was being offered by her counsellor. She preferred her practical, goal-focused approach. It had become clear in the two consultations that she was not so much depressed as understandably and appropriately angry and saddened by the breakup of her parents' marriage and upset about some rather high-handed treatment meted out by her insensitive father. She was prone to brief but intense outbursts of tears on arriving home in the evening. She was doing well at school and was full of energy and enthusiasm when talking about her friends and her future plans for university and a career. She had a good relationship with her mother. She came across as a young woman who was struggling with unexpected and testing events, but who would almost certainly have the resources within herself to win the battle. She pronounced herself to be fundamentally content and optimistic.

The boy in the first referral letter did not present as might have been expected from the description. He was a very depressed child. His omnipotence and defiance were paper thin and it was heart-rending to see the pained expression in his eyes as he sat, hunched, listening to his parents as they spoke of his many failings. His mother seemed particularly cold and unreachable. When the family therapist congratulated him on the way he was behaving in the meeting, he smiled weakly at her and then winced as his mother came back with a description of yet another recent misdemeanour. Of course, it was clear that his parents felt worn down by their inability to understand his behaviour and make things better. His inner feelings were well hidden beneath behaviour which provoked anger and depression in others, particularly in his parents and teachers. It was obvious to me in the family meeting because I had the opportunity to look on and listen, whilst my colleague asked careful questions. My colleague was at pains to convince him of her interest and open-mindedness.

The aim of this chapter is to look at depression from a psychoanalytic viewpoint and to offer clinical examples from both short- and long-term psychotherapy. The opening examples serve to illustrate that diagnosis is no simple matter. The word depression can be a handy catch-all for any number of states of mind. Similarly, genuine depression can be masked by an inordinate number of worrying or challenging behaviour patterns. For a psychoanalytic psychotherapist, depression is a condition of the person's internal world. It is a description of an individual's state when he feels his internal resources to be attacked or depleted. In extreme cases the fear may be that there is nothing life-enhancing inside and that the capacity to interact purposefully with the outside world has been lost.

It is, of course, a condition that is related to the external world in a very real sense. Depression can be reactive. Real events such as bereavement, redundancy, divorce, displacement and so on can precipitate any of us into a depression. For small children, events such as losing a friend, a favourite pet or a trusted teacher can do the same. Being bullied at school is a very common precipitating factor.

Therapists who underestimate the importance of external circumstances do so at their peril. Unemployment, exam failure, ill-health or homelessness do sap people's energy and confidence, and recovery may depend on real improvements happening outside the consulting room. For others the depression may endure long after external problems seem to be solved. In yet another group, the depression appears to come, as it were, out of the blue. Seen from the outside their life is full of interest, success and good relationships, and yet the depression is there and keeps recurring.

Depression is a condition that may be activated or reactivated by external events, but it is a condition of the internal world, rooted in the individual's object relations and, psychoanalysis would suggest, stemming from the interplay in early life between an individual's constitution and his primary relationships. The suggestion is not that early relationships that are good and nourishing provide a complete immunization against depression. The notion is, rather, that the introjection of good experiences and the establishment of strong internal objects (or parental representations) provides the individual with the internal structure on which to draw when depression threatens to throw things out of balance. In simple terms, our early experiences, and what we make of them, leave us more or less susceptible to depression and more or less able to deal with it.

Observation of infants has much to teach us about depression, as about so many other aspects of human growth, development and mental health (Miller *et al.*, 1989). We have only recently begun to talk in terms of babies being depressed and have questioned many of our assumptions about what is going on in the infant psyche. The so-called 'good' baby who never complains, sleeps well, and feeds moderately, may indeed be developing well. If the same baby shows little interest in people, and is slow to respond to talk, touch or laughter, there may be cause for concern. A protesting baby may be challenging to his parents but he or she is making a statement about being alive and having needs. A little frustration is a necessary element in all human learning and development. A baby whose every need is anticipated and met before she or he can even become aware of it, may become somewhat dulled. On the other hand, a baby whose protests are not heard and do not receive attention, may very well give up trying. There is obviously a balance to be achieved and most infants and parents rub along together in a 'good enough' sort of a way (Winnicott, 1960). Where a more passive baby meets a depressed mother, one can see that a cycle of flat, lifeless inter-action may be set in motion. These babies are, perhaps, more at risk when facing separation, loss and change, than are those who are well endowed at birth and are born to lively parents or caregivers.

Anne Alvarez (1992) writes very helpfully on this subject. She identi-fies 'reclamation' as an essential part of the psychotherapeutic technique, just as it is an essential component of normal maternal functioning, crucial to the child's emotional and cognitive development. She consid-ers the way in which mothers function as 'alerters, arousers and enliven-ers' of their babies and summarizes the child development research (Brazelton *et al.*, 1974; Trevarthen 1984; Stern 1985) which points to a rhythmical, cyclic interaction of mother and infant, involving approach and retreat, periods of quiet and periods of intensity. She rightly reminds us of the depression that is also present in children who are primarily deprived or are suffering from chronic neglect. In relation to therapeutic work with severely deprived, autistic or depressed children, Alvarez sees active pursuit of contact as the therapist's crucial function. There is a job to be done which involves convincing the child that there is a receptive object; a lively, interested mind making itself available. Where depression borders on despair she suggests that even the so-called defensive manoeuvres of omnipotence or hostility are to be respected as indicators of something lively and potentially creative surviving within the child. To be too quick to challenge these might be to rob the child of what little internal resilience he or she has.

Philip

Some children alert their parents and other adults to the fact that there is something wrong but do so in a way which disguises the real issues. This little boy's presenting problem was temper tantrums and his depression was held at bay by his all-consuming passion for aeroplanes so that loss and separation, which he could not manage for reasons that will become obvious, were avoided at all costs.

Philip's parents sought professional help when he was just four years old. He had been excluded from two nursery schools and a series of au pairs/nannies had come and gone. His tantrums were said to be outra-geous and his attacks on his baby sister violent and unrelenting. His parents spanked him and imposed sanctions. Punishments included being shut in his room for hours at a time and being sent to bed without supper. They made lengthy speeches to him, explaining why they had to teach him these lessons and what he could do to be the sort of son whom they would love and who would make them proud. It was all spelled out in calm, rational terms. One of the most potent bargaining chips between Philip and his parents was his access to 'his aeroplanes'. He had innumerable toys, models, books and posters on the subject and he was always hungry for more. His favourite treat was a trip to an Aircraft Museum or Air Show. His parents unwittingly fed into his obsession. They were impressed by his encyclopedic knowledge and encouraged relatives to send him planes on postcards and planes for his birthday and for Christmas. When they were exasperated with him and wanting to teach him the consequences of his actions, they deprived him of his planes. Philip came into treatment about a year after the family's arrival in the country. They were Australian but had been working in Singapore for some years. Ever since their marriage they had been moving from job to job and from country to country. For Philip, leaving Singapore meant leaving a long-established nanny. It became clear that nobody had really stopped to wonder about the impact of such an upheaval. When we asked about it, Philip's parents looked puzzled. 'What do you mean?' Slowly, over a number of appointments, we heard that the move had been sudden and unwelcome. Mrs C hated Britain; their first rented house here was horrible and they had moved on very quickly. She had given up a stimulating job in Singapore and now felt relatively housebound whereas Mr C travelled all over the world on business (in aeroplanes!) and was away much of the time. Mrs C was clearly very depressed and quite unable to recognize it. She did, in fact, have a job herself and was also away at intervals. We learned that Philip was not told in advance about their movements and his mother would often slip away without a word, believing that this was the kindest way to do it. When we asked about Philip's early history, we were met with the same incredulity. What was that to do with anything? They simply wanted to know how to teach him not to be so naughty. We eventually pieced some details together and built up a picture of a baby whose busy and well-meaning parents had been very remote. One particular image sticks in my mind: his father described how he would jog past the house at midday and he would wave and shout 'Hi son!' to Philip in his buggy.

When psychotherapy was offered, Mr and Mrs C were unsure about it. They wanted to know if I would be doing role play and setting up situations to provoke Philip into tantrums. They wanted to know whether the programme would include assessments of his progress. A skilled social worker colleague undertook weekly work with them alongside Philip's therapy and helped them to shift their thinking, so that when the next move came up (which, sadly, happened just eight months into the therapy) they approached it in a different way. They were beginning to recognize that their son was anxious about sudden changes and they did their best to prepare him.

Philip spent almost every minute of every session drawing aeroplanes. He would come in cheerfully, sit down, and take out a fresh piece of paper, already well into a description of what was to be today's chosen plane. Sometimes they were drawn in pieces, which were then painstakingly cut out, ready to be taped or glued together. His talk was all about planes and I spent the early weeks trying to achieve a balance between making sure I was not rejecting in my response and yet feeling that I had to find a way to make some space in the session for something else to develop, if at all possible. At first, my heart would lift if his gaze went to some other toy in his box, or if he began to tell me about something other than planes. As the weeks went on, my hopefulness gave way to passivity; I became unutterably bored. I was given an experience of waiting and hoping which I came to believe must have been very much his experience in relation to his parents; waiting for them to notice his distress and understand it. On one or two occasions he made an attempt at a game of throw and catch and I felt that he just did not know how to engage in this play. His actions were floppy and uncoordinated, in marked contrast to the high degree of manual dexterity he could display when drawing and manipulating scissors. If I was too enthusiastic in my response to something which was not a plane, he would recoil and rush straight back to his drawing, sometimes asking plaintively 'I'm a handsome little designer aren't I?'

For some time I saw his aeroplane world as being a refuge; the planes as his friends. They certainly were something through which he could engage his parents' interest. However, I began to see that it was much more complicated than that. The planes were adored and he found them exciting, but they were also dangerous and sometimes had to be placated, lest they crash or drop bombs or turn into sharks. These transformations occurred at unpredictable intervals and were quickly glossed over. As the months went by, he divided his plane population into 'German' and 'Allied' and we began to see some differentiation between what was safe and good and what was hostile and dangerous. I became somebody who had to be won over with lots of impressive plane talk, or somebody who would be so envious of his capacity to draw and his knowledge that I would attack; become an enemy plane. On one occasion, he was shutting me out with plane talk when a real plane passed noisily overhead. He ducked in terror and half acknowledged that he was expecting some sort of retaliatory attack.

Any holiday break or missed session would lead to a redoubling of his efforts to fill his mind and mine with planes. He would sometimes talk in grandiose terms about how, when he was a pilot, he would fly in through the window and land on my carpet whenever he chose. The separation at the end of sessions was dealt with by his taking his drawing or model away with him. No amount of interpretation could get him to contemplate leaving the concrete products of his session behind and short of wrestling them away from him, there was nothing I could do to impose this particular psychotherapy boundary. He left only a very few – those that were unfinished and those that had not turned out as he intended (Fig. 4.1).

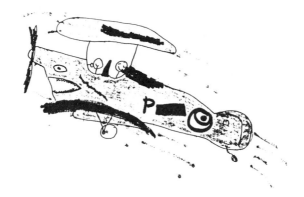

Figure 4.1: a drawing by Philip

Externally, things were improving. His parents were altering their management of him and succeeded in preparing him to start school, which he managed remarkably well. They resolved to be entirely neutral about planes, neither encouraging nor banning them. They tried, as I had in sessions, to be mildly bored by plane talk and much more enthusiastic about anything else. I felt that Philip picked up on this campaign and resisted it. When I expressed disappointment about him going straight into planes at the start of one session, he got up and threw the ball back and forth a few times! This was done as if it were an act of great generosity to a poor, plane-less being.

Philip was not a passive, uncomplaining child. Far from it. He was, however, a depressed child who was becoming full of despair about his own ability to interest and excite his rather unimaginative parents and to exert any control over his very unpredictable life. His therapy came to an end very prematurely and all too abruptly. His father was made redundant and then found a new job back in Australia and they packed up and left within three weeks. I had one session in which to say goodbye to Philip.

He came into the room in the normal way and I felt cruel at having to spell out that this was to be our last meeting. Almost immediately, he lost his composure. The first attempt at a drawing was cast aside, then the second, and then he rounded on me and shouted that it was all my fault. He could no longer manage the pencil, the tip broke, the sharpener fell to the floor. He scribbled angrily and ranted at me that I should shut up and leave him alone. Then came 'I'll never say goodbye!' and 'I hate you. You and your damned designs!' He suddenly seemed small and vulnerable in a way I had not felt before and I wanted to comfort him. However, he had spun away and was sitting under the sink counter, clinging to an upright pole support and saying that he was not going, not going to say goodbye, and I should just go away; I should go and leave him in peace. He then muttered, 'I'll never be any good at anything.' I felt devastated as I sat with him and I had to fight back the tears.

I tried to talk about overwhelming feelings and it being difficult to do his usual drawings today and about the importance of being able to let me see how he was feeling. I did not think he was hearing me. I then felt immensely impressed by this boy's resilience as he got up and came back to sit at the table and start again. He started hopefully but again it went wrong and this time he screwed up the paper and threw it out of the window and onto the flat roof outside, 'There! Now it will stay there for ever.' He was shaking from head to foot and I began to feel that further interpretation would drive him wild and that there was nothing I could do with words to relieve his distress. I felt I had to help him regain some sort of equilibrium before the end of the session and so, with just a few minutes left, I set about helping him build his plane.

We managed this together and I then said my goodbyes and took him through to where his mother was waiting with the social worker. She admired the plane and he told her that it had not been easy but that he had managed it. 'That's good, Philip, try, try and try again. That's a good big boy.' When we all said goodbye, Philip could not look at me but went out thanking the social worker for an elastic band she had supplied. He almost ran from the room.

I was later told that Philip had set off down the stairs but had then returned to show his plane to the staff at reception. They had admired it and he had said 'Miss Youell taught me how to make this kind.'

This postscript to the session, more than anything, left me with a sense of some hope for Philip. My feeling is that he will continue to strive and protest and, provided his parents can be helped to think about their passionate, stormy son, he may do well and be able, eventually, to leave the planes behind. His parents' matter-of-factness and stolid denial that the moves and changes were difficult for all of them, was challenged by Philip's strong expression of his needs. He forced them to stop and look at what was going on. I felt less optimistic about his younger sister. She was brought into one meeting, asleep in a baby rocker. When she awoke, in a strange room full of strange adults, she showed no distress, no curiosity, and did not really look around for her mother. She simply waited.

Simon

My second example, in contrast to that of Philip, is of a 17-year-old boy, referred to the clinic for help with a reactive depression. What emerged was a picture of how much current events were resonating with past experiences and evoking uncomfortable and unresolved aspects of his early life.

Simon went to seek help from his general practitioner shortly before the end of his first year in the sixth form. He had decided to repeat the year and wanted the GP to back this decision with a medical statement. He felt that events within the family had been such that his work had suffered. He was, in fact, taking days and weeks off at a time. When I heard the story, I felt that this was not surprising. I was impressed that he could get himself to go in at all. Simon's mother was an alcoholic. His father had lived with this, with apparent fortitude, for 10 or more years but had quite suddenly left the home to live with a new partner. He was now saying that he had served his sentence and was not doing any more. He did not want Simon, or his daughter (15), to join him. His new partner had two young children and that was more than enough for one household.

Simon was stunned. In addition to his private shock and sorrow, he was having to cope with the public disgrace. His father worked at the school and gave up his job along with the marriage. The separation also meant that Simon and his mother and sister would soon have to move into temporary accommodation for homeless families. When he came to his first session, Simon poured out massive amounts of detail about events and about the repercussions on his relationships at school, with friends and with his girlfriend. It took several appointments before either of us felt that he had sufficient time to tell his story. He recognized that he was very depressed and thought that once his story was shared he would be able to motivate himself to get back to school, back to studying, and back to his normal life. The last thing he wanted was to become dependent on talking to a 'professional'. He started taking anti-depressants and hated himself for it. What if he became dependent on them?

Simon attended sessions for exactly one year. He stopped when he had successfully negotiated his first-year A-level exams. He had also become a little more accepting of his father's new situation and a little more realistic about the very slim chances of his mother managing to keep to a detoxification programme. At the beginning of our contact, he was adamant that she was not drinking, however obvious the evidence was to the contrary. What took Simon entirely by surprise was the way in which these trying events stirred up memories and feelings from the past. He found himself having dreams which he recognized as being the same dreams that had recurred in his childhood. He needed his bedroom light on at night and he was revisited by a phobia of cuddly toys that had plagued him as a small boy. He started to idealize his girl-friend and then became very demanding and possessive, seeing betrayal in her every action. He found himself thinking of early friendships and realizing just how manipulative he had felt himself to be in his determination to keep his 'special friend'. He felt renewed surges of rivalry about his younger sister and felt that it was all happening again; she was the favourite, she received much better treatment than he.

He hated his potential step-siblings with enormous energy; they were beneath contempt. He found oedipal feelings and memories revived, deeply disturbed by his father's sexual activity and confused by finding himself, as it were, in sole possession of his mother. Simon was deeply depressed. None of his internal objects seemed to be intact; all was in flux and confusion to the extent that he felt paralysed and very detached from ordinary life and its everyday concerns.

He admitted to suffering terrible obsessional symptoms and constructing elaborate rituals for himself, all designed to avert disaster and detoxify his own very destructive impulses. He would, for instance, wish his father's girlfriend harm, and then quickly tell himself that if he crossed the road three times before he reached the next lamppost the wish would not come true. He finished with his girlfriend and became almost housebound for a time, convinced that everyone was talking about him and hating him. He missed some sessions. My attempts to think about this, and other material, in the transference, were largely rebuffed. I was not an important figure; simply a counsellor doing a job of work (I was never acknowledged as being a psychotherapist) and he could take it or leave it. What he was talking about was real. They were homeless, his father had rejected him, and his mother was drunk and full of self-pity. Enough, he insisted, to make anyone depressed.

He was, however, very caught up in the process of revisiting and reexamining the childhood he had always idealized. He had thought that his parents were the perfect couple, the perfect parents. He had, he realized, shut out the fears and doubts that had first pressed in on him when he was about nine or ten. He had refused to notice the bottles, the sickness, the rows. He had refused to notice that trips out were taken with either one or the other parent, rarely with both. He was sure that when he and his sister were little it had not been like that. They had been a very happy family and he had felt safe and loved. He then had a dream that he said was very familiar to him; he thought it had started as a sort of waking dream when he was quite young, and was linked in some way to a hamster that was lost in the house and never found.

He is in bed and there are hundreds and hundreds of hamsters coming out from under his bed and under the wardrobe. They are all furry and they keep multiplying. He shouts for his parents and they come and start to kill some of the hamsters but then more appear. They are soft and fluffy but somehow terrifying and have big eyes.

We examined this dream together and the variations he could remember. He said that he was terrified but did feel pleased in the dream that his parents had responded to his cries, as if it were confirmation that they did care and that they would protect him. He said he had never looked under his wardrobe for fear that he would find the remains of his lost hamster. He had not allowed a mouse trap to be set in the house, fearing that the mouse they had seen might be some sort of mutation, offspring of the pet animal. He was very interested in my suggestion that the duplicating hamsters might represent rival babies; children which his parents might get together to produce. He immediately made an association with his cuddly toy phobia, saying that they have such hard, accusing eyes, looking at him with hatred. He remembered how he used to beg his parents to reassure him that they did not need more children.

He was embarrassed at these memories but was rather relieved to be able to think about them. He could see that when he looked at the threatening eyes of the hamsters, what he was seeing was a reflection of his own hostility. He was then able to acknowledge his fear of his own aggression in the current situation. He said that he felt guilty about being so possessive and demanding of first one parent and then the other but he had never been able to stop himself and it was how he felt again now. He wanted to force his father to put him first.

Very slowly and painfully, he put together a lot of half-memories and parts of dreams and faced a few very distressing truths. I believe he found the safety he needed to do this within the containing setting of the therapy sessions. There had also been a recognition of something akin to a concerned parental couple, in the shape of myself and the GP. I had been very worried about Simon prior to a holiday break. He had missed a session with no message. I wrote to his doctor who took it upon himself to summon Simon in for a consultation. When I saw a copy of this letter to Simon I felt very worried. He would surely experience this as a breach of confidentiality on my part and as an unwarranted interference by his GP. To my surprise he returned after the break, saying that he had been taken aback by the summons but had secretly felt rather pleased by the idea that we had got together to worry about him and to make provision for him.

Simon slowly became better able to recognize his parents' short-comings and, as he did so, he felt the beginnings of something much more forgiving. When they were no longer the 'fallen-angel' parents who had betrayed him, he was able to allow for the fact that they were responsible for their own actions (that he could not stop his mother drinking) and that his father had a right to make choices about his own future. Simon, in turn, began to feel that he could move on, pass his A-levels and go away to University. He was still very worried about dependency, cutting the contact with me a year before his departure from the area but acknowledging that, in this way, he would feel in control and able to return to me, or somebody else, should he need to do so in the future. He was a boy who was not without internal resources. It did seem that he must have had something good and nourishing from his parents when he was an infant. Recent traumatic events had resonated with less resolved aspects of his experience and he had been thrown off balance. He was, however, able to make use of an opportunity to think about and understand some of these issues and rediscover his own inner resources. He became more accepting of reality, which included recognizing the hamster-child within himself.

Beth

My third example is chosen as an illustration of the way in which, for some patients, being able to be in touch with depression, and to acknowledge it for what it is, is actually a step towards health. When Beth came into intensive psychotherapy, she was not depressed: she was persecuted and furious, full of righteous indignation and hatred for her objects. In Kleinian terms, she was locked in the paranoid-schizoid position, with no real feelings of concern for others and little capacity to take responsibility for her actions (Klein, 1946).

Beth started psychotherapy with me three times a week when she was twelve. This was my first contact with her, but she was no newcomer to the clinic. Her family had first attended when she was five and had been back and forth in various combinations for various brief and less-brief interventions ever since. Beth had been in once-weekly individual psychotherapy and her sister had been seen intensively. Her parents had been seen as a couple for some years. She was now asking to be seen again and the decision was reached that she would be offered intensive treatment or nothing; the 'dipping in and out' had to come to an end. I include all this detail because it is important in trying to describe the way in which I quickly came to feel that Beth was going through the motions of being in therapy. She was well versed in the language and had all the 'right' reactions to events such as cancellations, holiday breaks, evidence of the existence of my other patients, and so on. She attended every session; she expressed anger, curiosity, envy and so on, but there was something unconvincing about it.

Looking back, I think she asked to see a therapist again because she did not know what else to do, or how to find relief from what she was feeling. She was friendless, overweight and extremely angry.

In the early months, sessions were filled up with long, complicated descriptions of events at home: rows that seemed to have escalated out of nothing and which always left Beth feeling misunderstood and ill-used. She seemed to want to prove her case, like a barrister in court, and then to polish up her sense of grievance. I was to be convinced that she was in the right and that her own, sometimes appalling, behaviour was entirely to be condoned in the circumstances. I was asked, again and again, to agree that she had been unfairly treated and that her hated sister had 'got away Scot free'. She would sit with angry tears pouring down her face as she told me the latest episode and it was difficult to hold onto the fact that she was seeking justice over an issue such as whose turn it was to sit in the front seat of the car.

School was another battleground in which she, Beth, was presented as the innocent victim of teachers' sadism and other girls' perfidy. She would construct elaborate schemes to trap girls into being her partner and would nurse her wounds when it did not turn out the way she had planned. If somebody showed some interest in getting to know her, she would test their loyalty and commitment beyond what they could endure. Girls who let her down repeatedly or left her out of their arrangements became the subjects of complicated retaliatory campaigns.

I wondered how I could ever make any inroads into this mountain of bitterness and resentment. While she talked in those early sessions, she drew hundreds of 'models', tall, skinny young women with long blonde hair, stiletto heels and vacuous expressions. This, she said, was what she wanted to be: beautiful, popular, sexually desirable and rich. If only she were not so fat and did not have such a horrible family. In the face of all this it may seem surprising that I quickly came to feel a very real concern and sympathy for her. There were times when her melodramatic sobs became absolutely real and heart-rending. There were lighter moments too. She had somehow retained a sense of humour and showed flashes of insight about other people which led me to feel hopeful about her ability, in the long term, to look at herself. She did have some cause to complain. Her parents were at war with each other and her sister was overindulged by her father. Limits were not set. Beth seemed to be very porous to the emotional states that her parents were incapable of holding in themselves or on behalf of their two daughters. As in the example of Philip, I felt Beth's anger to be linked with protest and a sense of hope. She firmly believed that things should be better. In many ways, she was the most hopeful member of her family.

Early in the therapy I appeared in two waking fantasies. In the first, I was sitting behind her in the cinema, 'snogging' with my boyfriend. In the second, I was seen hanging out of the window of an old Ford Cortina, chewing, swearing and flicking ash into the gutter. I came to see that this was the sort of object she expected to be offered. She expressed astonishment at my 'computer' memory but saw this as a bit of a circus trick and not as evidence of any real interest or concern. I was somebody who followed a therapy 'rule-book' in sessions and then turned my back and got on with my ordinary life as a foul-mouthed, tarty young woman. Little evidence of maternal capacity. It should be added that the figure described was also not at all like her actual mother, but like the models she constantly drew.

As time progressed, Beth came to depend on the fact that I knew about so much of her life and she liked the fact that I remembered details. I became somebody who was allowed to challenge her and even to tease her a little. She found me to be friendly and was relieved, I think, that I did not allow her to get away with her more extravagant complaints. I was permitted to see that she had another version of herself. If she did not cling to an idea of herself as an innocent victim of everybody else's abusive ways she could only see herself as beneath contempt and beyond hope. She was disgusting. I learned that it helped if I reminded her from time to time of her actual abilities, keeping the ordinarily competent young teenager in mind when she was trying to make me agree with her totally negative, totally worthless version of herself.

I became more and more in touch with the vulnerable part of her, and better able to circumnavigate the minefield that the warring part of her would sometimes lay in my path. However, after a sequence of honest and touching sessions, I would be cast down by the sudden reappearance of the brittle, unforgiving Beth. This would often follow a sudden recurrence of family warfare at home.

By the second year, Beth was working very hard in sessions. She brought dreams, made links, told me what she had been thinking about between sessions, and was genuinely interested in the work. She was friendly and appreciative. I was idealized somewhat as kind, thoughtful, and utterly reliable. She was relishing the work and then the holiday break impinged in a way which was very unexpected. She was not able to verbalize it in a straightforward way but it was obvious that, for the first time, she really minded. After the break, her therapy entered a new phase and there were parallel but very different changes in her external life. In therapy, she had a new problem; she was angry with me. Allowing herself to feel this fully, or to express it to me, was impossible for her. She did not want to have complicated, mixed feelings about me. She began to cancel sessions and to talk about stopping. All interest and commitment was projected into me. She told me, very politely, that she did not want me to lose income and she did not want to be ungrateful, but she wanted to try life without the clinic. (It was always 'the clinic' so as to keep it impersonal and distant.) It seemed that she was beginning to realize that to continue with therapy would involve acknowledging the importance of the relationship. I talked to her about ambivalence and she made a 'poster' of the word in the last session of the term.

At around that time she had an experience of feeling sudden empathy for her troubled sister. She still judged her behaviour to be outrageous but she was suddenly, although briefly, overwhelmed by feelings of sorrow at her predicament. She wanted to comfort her. It was shocking to her to discover that her hatred was more than tinged with love and pity. Again, I feel that it is worth emphasizing the development of a different, more concerned relationship with the part of herself that she had projected into her sister and hated for so long.

Externally, there was what might be described as a 'flight into health'. Beth suddenly began referring to 'friends' and telling me about group activities at school and gatherings at weekends. She did well in exams. She went on school journeys. She was in demand. This, of course, enabled her to complain, more truthfully, that therapy was a hindrance to her developing other aspects of her life. Contact was reduced to one session per week and was maintained at that level for the following two years. The therapy was sometimes attacked by Beth's 'forgetfulness' but even at the worst times (when the demands of friends, school events, holidays, TV programmes and so forth always came first) contact was maintained and the work continued.

The agenda, as Beth saw it, had changed. She no longer worried about whether she would make friends: she had a large group of friends of both sexes, as well as one 'best friend'. She was even beginning to lose weight. To some extent, she had given up hope of changing things within her family and had separated herself from them in many day-to-day, practical ways. She had become conscious of the fact that she was depressed. She became very depressed and I was worried about her. Just at the point when I was seriously concerned about her suicidal intentions, she rallied a little and told me that depression was awful but at least she knew what she was battling with.

I would suggest that the therapeutic experience had slowly and painfully challenged Beth's omnipotence and put her in touch with depressive feelings (Klein, 1940). The structure was containing. She felt that she was allowed – indeed encouraged – to make contact with, and express, the full range of, her feelings, and that she was not judged. It was, I hope, the opposite of the courtroom she was so keen to create. I believe it was also, for her, a prototypical experience of friendly contact. There were times when I had to hold all the concern, all the interest, all the memory, all the reliability, and all the depression. The fact that I did so, over such a long period of time, and remained 'friendly' in the process, helped her, I think, to develop her own capacities to take on more and more of the work for herself.

In a recent review meeting, Beth told me that she is suffering terrible bouts of depression. As she put it: 'Life can really be shit.' She also told me that she does not really understand it, but she feels 'Sort of OK.'

Conclusion

Depression in children and young people manifests itself in many different ways. The way in which it manifests itself is partly dependent on the child's stage of development and on the ways she or he has developed for managing the pain and fear involved in loss and change. Parents and other concerned adults can be deceived by challenging and puzzling behaviour patterns, and they can be drawn into playing a part that matches the child's internal figures, often becoming punishing or ineffective and failing to see the underlying primary depression.

For some children, recognizing depression for what it is can be a very important stage in moving towards greater health. When depression is identified, experienced and contained in the psychotherapeutic setting, the sense of relief and the ensuing growth of trust in strengthened internal structures can lead to a more hopeful developmental path.

References

Alvarez A (1992) Live Company. London and New York: Tavistock/Routledge.

Klein M (1940) Mourning and its relation to manic depressive states. In Love, Guilt and Reparation. The Writings of Melanie Klein. Vol II. London: Hogarth.

Klein M (1946) Notes on some schizoid mechanisms. In Envy and Gratitude. The Writings of Melanie Klein. Vol III. London: Hogarth.

Miller L, Rustin M, Rustin M, Shuttleworth J (1989) Closely Observed Infants. London: Duckworth & Co.

Winnicott D (1960) Ego distortion in terms of true and false self. In The Maturational Processes and the Facilitating Environment. London: Hogarth.

Chapter 5
Cognitive-Behavioural Therapy for Depression In Children and Adolescents

MARY EVANS AND ANN MURPHY

History

Cognitive-behavioural therapy for depression developed from a combination of the cognitive therapy first used by psychoanalysts Beck (1963) and Ellis (1962), and elements of behavioural therapy. Beck (1979) traced the origins of cognitive therapy to the stoic philosophers and quotes Epictetus: 'men are disturbed not by things but by the view which they take of them.'

Seligman's theory of learned helplessness (Seligman, 1975) and attribution theory (Abramson *et al.*, 1978) have been important influences on cognitive-behavioural therapy. Meichenbaum and Goodman's (1971) description of 'self-talk' is another influence. 'Self-talk' develops in young children as a result of the instructions they receive about their behaviour from external influences such as parents. They gradually learn to control their behaviour through their own verbal instructions and this is eventually internalized to silent inner speech.

Theoretical basis

Cognitive-behavioural therapy has become a standard treatment for mild to moderate adult depression and has been shown in clinical trials to be as effective as antidepressant medication (Kovacs *et al.*, 1981). It is an active, directive, time-limited, structured approach (Beck, 1979) in which cognitive and behavioural theories and the internal and external world of the child are integrated (Meichenbaum, 1977). A central assumption of this approach is that a person's affect and behaviour are largely determined by the way in which he or she interprets the world. Thoughts, or cognitions, are derived from attitudes and assumptions, that have developed through previous experience. Those beliefs that lead to negative emotions and unhelpful behaviours are challenged in cognitive behavioural therapy.

Schemata

Ellis, using Rational Emotive Therapy, uses the letters 'A', 'B' and 'C' to describe elements of the mental processes leading to depression: 'A' is the activating event, 'B' the belief and 'C' the consequences. People are often unaware of the 'B' components of the process and therapy is directed towards uncovering them – helping the patient to see the undesirable consequences of irrational beliefs so that she or he can change them. These core beliefs, or basic assumptions, are termed 'schemata' by Beck. In individuals prone to depression, schemata tend to centre on themes such as, 'for me to be happy, people must like me/agree with me at all times', 'to be happy, I must be loved', 'if I make a mistake, I must be a total failure' or 'if I do not do everything perfectly, I am worthless'. A child with this basic assumption may become depressed after failing an exam: 'I've failed, I'll always fail, I'm worthless'.

Stark *et al.* (1991) use the concept of schemata to explain the consistency seen in an individual's thoughts, feelings and behaviour. Schemata determine how a child codes the stimuli and categorizes the information with which he or she is confronted. Schemata are thought to be organized in a hierarchical fashion with core schemata at the top. The nature of an individual's core schemata will influence secondary schemata and automatic thoughts.

Automatic thoughts

The depressed individual tends to see himself, the world and the future in a negative light; he or she is 'worthless', the world is 'bleak' and the future 'hopeless'. Beck (1979) termed this 'the cognitive triad'. Much of the depressed person's thinking centres around these depressogenic themes. Thinking is categorized by negative or 'automatic' thoughts which are believable to the patient, autonomous, and he or she is often unaware of them. For example a girl became very sad when her friend passed her without saying 'hello'. She believed that her friend's behaviour was the reason for her low mood. In therapy she realized that it was the thought 'Sarah doesn't want to know me any more, I must be a really terrible person' that made her sad. In cognitive-behavioural therapy the automatic thoughts are identified and challenged. It is important that the child learns to evaluate himself or herself less harshly and more realistically.

Cognitive errors

The depressed person makes a number of errors in thinking which maintain the negative view of the self, the world and the future (the cognitive triad), despite evidence that throws doubt upon these negative thoughts (Beck, 1979). Cognitive errors are the result of maladaptive schemata and give rise to automatic thoughts that confirm the pessimistic outlook. The systematic errors described by Beck include:

- *Arbitrary inference* or 'jumping to conclusions'. A conclusion is drawn despite lack of evidence to support it or despite evidence against it. 'Gemma didn't phone today, she doesn't want to be friends any more.' (Gemma was out with her parents.)
- *Selective abstraction.* Focusing on a part of a situation, taken out of context, and ignoring other aspects of the situation. For example, a girl might think 'Jim thinks I'm ugly' when Jim has asked her friend to go out.
- *Overgeneralization.* Drawing a general conclusion on the basis of one piece of evidence. 'I got C for my maths exam; I'm useless at school work' (despite having good marks in all other subjects).
- *Magnification and minimization.* Overemphasizing or underemphasizing the importance of an event so that its significance is distorted: 'I got into the school football team, anyone who was interested in football could have done so, it's a poor team' (having tried hard to get into the team).
- *Personalization.* Relating external events to oneself when there is no evidence to suggest that they have anything to do with oneself. 'Mum and Dad are always fighting because of me.'
- *Dichotomous thinking* ('black and white thinking'). Categorizing things in an 'all or nothing' way – for example, 'I had an argument with Mum last night; I'm a totally bad daughter.'
- *Catastrophizing.* Here disaster is predicted when there is no evidence that disaster is imminent. 'Dad's late home; he's had an accident and been killed.' (This cognitive error is associated with anxiety.)

Cognitive errors in children and adolescents

The thoughts of depressed children are dominated by a negative view of the self, the world and the future (Stark *et al.*, 1991). The thoughts occur autonomously and are believed. Depressed children, like depressed adults, misinterpret information from the environment and internal world in a way which serves to maintain this negative view (Haley *et al.*, 1985). One study showed that they see themselves as less able than their non-depressed peers, even though their teachers noted no difference (Kendall *et al.*, 1990).

Depressed youth have a more depressogenic attributional style than non-depressed controls (Kaslow, *et al.*, 1988; Kendall, 1993). Their locus of control has also been shown to be more external (Mullins *et al.*,

1985). Depressed children make more internal, global and stable attributions for failure and more external, unstable and specific attributions for success (Kaslow *et al.*, 1984; Curry and Craighead, 1990; Seligman *et al.*, 1984). The depressed child is thus likely to interpret positive events as occurring in response to external factors over which he or she has no control and negative events as entirely her or his own fault.

The self-esteem of depressed children is low (Asarnow *et al.*, 1987; Kendall, 1993). In a task requiring copying they set more stringent standards, punished themselves more and rewarded themselves less than controls (Kaslow *et al.*, 1984). Depressed children display many of the cognitive distortions described in adults (Beck, 1979). They overgeneralize their predictions of negative outcomes, catastrophize the consequences of negative events, incorrectly take personal responsibility for negative outcomes and attend selectively to the negative features of an event (Kendall *et al.*, 1990).

Depressed children and adolescents also display some deficiencies in problem solving (Kendall, 1993) with high rates of depressogenic strategies (Asarnow *et al.*, 1987) and low rates of impersonal problem solving (Mullins *et al.*, 1985). Adolescent females who have attempted suicide have been found to perceive negative situations as their fault, as unchangeable, and as pervading their life. They also have deficiencies in problem solving (Rotheram-Borus *et al.*, 1990).

Kempton *et al.* (1994) looked at cognitive distortions in adolescents with depression, conduct disorder and substance abuse. Adolescents with a dual diagnosis of conduct disorder and depression, or who were comorbid for all three diagnoses, made similar cognitive distortions to those with pure depression. It was suggested that cognitive-based therapies aimed at depressive cognitions may be useful in these adolescents. This is relevant in view of the high rate of comorbidity of depression with other disorders such as conduct disorder (Kazdin, 1989; Harrington, 1991).

Cognitive distortions and cognitive deficiencies

Beck describes the dysfunctional, automatic or negative thoughts that perpetuate (and some would maintain cause) depression. Kendall distinguishes between cognitive distortions and cognitive deficiencies (Kendall, 1991, 1993). Cognitive deficiencies occur when young people do not think or engage in careful information processing in circumstances where this would be useful. For instance, an impulsive child, asked to bake a cake in class, throws all the ingredients in together without waiting for instructions and is disappointed with the resulting pancake. Cognitive distortions, by contrast, involve thinking in a biased way. In the same situation a depressed child is sure he or she is useless at baking, predicts failure, and may never get past the stage of weighing the ingredients. The difference is that between acting without thinking (not enough thought) and actions that follow misguided thinking (too much unhelpful thought).

The two types of cognitive error require different treatment strategies. Cognitive distortions need first to be identified and the dysfunctional thought corrected. For cognitive deficiencies, cognitive-behavioural therapy is directed at stopping non-thoughtful actions and encouraging the development of thoughtful problem solving. Children with internalizing disorders typically suffer cognitive distortions, whilst impulsive children show cognitive deficiencies. Aggressive children display both types of cognitive error. Consider the child who, when accidentally knocked by another, assumes that the action is deliberate and lashes out without stopping to consider the consequences.

Outcome research

There have been several studies looking at the efficacy of cognitive-behavioural therapy with depressed young people.

Reynolds and Coats (1986), in a school-based study, compared cognitive-behavioural intervention, relaxation training and a waiting-list control in 30 moderately depressed adolescents. Both active treatments produced significant reductions in depressive symptoms and the effect was maintained at the five-week follow-up.

Stark, Reynolds and Kaslow (1987) compared self-control, behavioural problem solving, and a waiting list control in a school-based study involving 29 children with moderate to severe depression. At the post-treatment follow-up, and again at the eight-week follow-up, both active groups had significantly improved.

In another school-based study, Stark et al. (1991) compared cognitive-behavioural therapy and traditional counselling. Twenty-four children were divided between the two treatments. At the post-treatment follow-up, cognitive-behavioural therapy was superior. In reviewing this study, Harrington (1992) suggested that this may indicate a specific therapeutic mechanism for cognitive-behavioural therapy. However the effect was not maintained at the seven-month follow-up.

Lewinsohn et al. (1990) found significant improvement among adolescents with dysthymia or major depression who were treated with a group based social skills training programme. It was suggested that increasing social skills helps a depressed young person to gain more positive reinforcement and that this will relieve the depression. Concurrent parental groups (that is, parallel group therapy sessions for the parents held at the same time) did not significantly improve the results.

Fine et al. (1989, 1991) noted that, in adolescents, there is an inverse relationship between knowledge of social skills and level of depression.

A therapeutic discussion group and social skills training group involving 66 depressed 14 to 17 year olds were compared. Both treatments were effective. Immediately post group, the therapeutic support group showed significantly less depression and a greater increase in self-concept, but at nine months the social skills group had caught up. It was noted that the therapeutic support group provided a supportive atmosphere of encouragement, cohesion and opportunities for self-expression and that this supportive atmosphere may be a necessary component for depressed youngsters to approach a more cognitive task like social skills. The social skills group focused on developing new skills to apply outside the group. It was suggested that there is a latency period in the successful utilization of such skills and their effect on depression and that prelearned skills may be more easily used once mood has begun to lift.

There is evidence that cognitive-behavioural therapy may be effective in preventing depression in young people identified as being at risk. Clarke *et al.* (1995) compared group cognitive therapy with 'usual care' in a school sample of adolescents with raised levels of depressive symptoms but no current affective diagnosis. Of 150 subjects, at 12 months, 14.5% of the treatment group were depressed, compared with 25.7% of the controls and the difference was statistically significant.

In a meta-analysis, Dulak *et al.* (1991) found that cognitive-behavioural approaches were almost twice as effective in children who could be assumed to have reached formal operational thinking (Piaget, 1977), aged around 11–13 years, when compared with younger children. The study concluded that cognitive-behavioural therapy was equally effective in all types of childhood problems, at all degrees of severity, regardless of the components that constituted the treatment. In the most frequently studied group (7–11 year olds), treatment gains were sustained at follow-up, which took place after an average of 4 months.

Until now, much of the research has been based on non-clinical samples. More recent projects such as Vostanis and Harrington (1994), however, aim to evaluate cognitive-behavioural therapy for clinical samples of depressed children and adolescents.

Cognitive-behavioural therapy in practice

The therapeutic alliance

As with other psychotherapies, the relationship between child and therapist is vital in cognitive-behavioural therapy. The therapist must respond to the child with genuineness, warmth and unconditional positive regard, but the therapist is more active than in the dynamic therapies and this can be an advantage in treating children and adolescents who find silence difficult. Wilkes *et al.* (1988) noted the importance of the therapeutic alliance when treating adolescents who may be coming to therapy against their will. Dysfunctional beliefs such as the idea that they have been sent for therapy as a punishment, or that the therapist can read their minds, must be addressed. Issues concerning transference are therefore not ignored. Kendall (1993) describes the 'posture of the therapist'. The spirit is questioning; the therapist does not have all the answers but is going on a voyage of discovery with the child to find out about him or herself and his or her thoughts and problems. The therapist does not dictate but has some ideas that the young person might find useful to try out. A collaborative approach is used (Beck, 1979). A team atmosphere is created; the child is educated about the cognitive-behavioural model of depression and together the child and the therapist see how well the child fits the model. Beck recommends the 'empirical' approach; hypotheses are made and experiments done to test them. Deductive reasoning is used. The aim is to enable the child to think things out for herself or himself and to develop problem-solving skills (Kendall, 1993). Often the therapist will use modelling as a way of enabling the child to recognize and challenge maladaptive affect, cognitions and behaviour.

Frequent use of summarizing and feedback from the child ensures that his or her viewpoint has been understood, that child and therapist are talking about the same things, and that the child finds the session useful. It is important that the therapist is non-judgemental; a neutral stance is taken and the inner experiences of the child are not dismissed. Humour can be a very useful therapeutic tool (Beck, 1979). This will obviously be more appropriate and spontaneous for some therapists; it is essential that rapport has been established and that the child does not think that he or she is 'being laughed at'. One example of the use of humour would be to exaggerate the child's thinking – for example, 'so you think that because you weren't picked you are an awful football player ... that bad ... the worst football player the world has ever seen?' The child may then see that this is absurd and recognize the inconsistencies in the beliefs. The cognitive-behavioural therapist seeks to create an atmosphere in which the dysfunctional thoughts of the child can be modified using behavioural experiments and deductive reasoning. A further goal of therapy is to modify or replace the unhelpful basic assumptions or schemata of the young person (Beck, 1979). Kendall (1991) has described this as 'building a coping template' to replace the existing one. For instance, a child who has the schema 'to be worthwhile I must succeed at all things' may recover from the present depression with the help of cognitive-behavioural treatment. Negative thoughts about always failing can be challenged and evidence can be gathered to show that the child is good at many things. If, however, the child's underlying schemata remain the same then he or she will be vulnerable to depression following future failures. It is harder for the child and therapist to build a 'coping template' than to modify a dysfunctional thought and it often includes cognitive work and behavioural experiments combined with affective experiences. Affect is important, as a situation with a high degree of emotion attached to it will be more likely to produce a change in the cognitive structure (Kendall, 1991). Moreover, early negative experiences often result in dysfunctional thinking. It is important that, if possible, therapy should continue until the underlying dysfunctional schemata have been modified and it should not terminate too soon. The reasons for this can be explained to the patient who may no longer be depressed and may feel no need of further therapy.

Engaging the depressed child or adolescent

Problems that can occur in the process of cognitive-behavioural therapy due to the symptoms of the depressed child have been discussed by Stark *et al.* (1991). Social withdrawal makes it difficult for the child to interact with the therapist and this makes it harder to establish a collaborative approach. There may also be a difficulty if the child becomes overdependent on the therapist. Hopelessness may make the child unlikely to try with therapy or complete homework as he or she may believe that nothing will work. If memory or concentration is impaired, if the child is tired or is unable to make decisions, this may make it hard to attend to therapy or homework.

It is especially important to engage the depressed child or adolescent who may be coming to therapy reluctantly. This can be difficult with a depressed child who predicts that treatment will fail. The child is likely to be quiet, and the therapist must work hard to find out information. Anhedonia and boredom are further barriers as the child can find therapy itself boring and his or her tolerance is low. It is important to make therapy fun, but this may not be easy with an anhedonic child. As Stark *et al.* (1991) suggest, a positive affective atmosphere in which the child is rewarded is helpful. The therapist should convey a sense of concern and hope whilst actively listening to the child.

Structure of therapy

Cognitive-behavioural therapy is probably best suited to older children and adolescents (Durlak *et al.*, 1991), but it has also been recommended for children of 5 years and over (Ronen, 1992).

Cognitive-behavioural therapy for depressed children and adolescents usually involves eight-to-twelve sessions, lasting from half an hour to one hour, and has been delivered in individual or group format. It is often helpful to have follow-up or booster sessions after therapy has finished. The individual sessions are structured as follows:

(1) *Setting the agenda.* Child and therapist together decide what topics are to be worked on during the session, the techniques that will be used and the goals of the session. The problems usually include matters that have been troubling the child. Questions are asked so that a detailed understanding of the problem and its components can be gained.

(2) *Review.* The child and therapist review what has happened since last session, including homework assignments.

(3) *Working through the day's problems and/or introducing new ideas.* Agenda items are tackled. Summaries are made throughout and feedback is sought.

(4) *Setting homework.* Suitable homework is decided collaboratively between child and therapist.

The predictable form of the sessions provides safe boundaries. These can be helpful in engaging a depressed child or adolescent who may find less structured psychotherapies threatening.

Homework is an integral part of cognitive-behavioural therapy. It has been shown with adults that patients who regularly carry out homework tasks do best and, specifically, that improvement is maintained after therapy (Beck, 1979). Our experience in group and individual work supports this. It is important that the child understands the reasons for doing homework, that she or he is involved in deciding what homework to do, and that any possible obstacles to its completion are explored. For instance, if the homework includes self-reward with a biscuit for recording a negative thought, parents need to allow access to the biscuit tin. It is important to involve parents and carers in therapy. This may vary from explaining the nature and purpose of cognitive-behavioural therapy, when the child is seen individually, to active involvement of parents as 'co-therapists' who can reinforce the techniques between sessions. Many children, seen in clinical settings, will also be involved in family work.

A variety of techniques can be used, either to suit the individual child or at different stages of therapy. Initially, and with younger or more severely depressed children, the emphasis will tend to be on behavioural tasks. With less depressed and older children and adolescents, more cognitive techniques are used. As a child gains formal operational thought and is able to make abstractions and see several possibilities in a given situation, cognitive-behavioural therapy can progress more along the lines described by Beck (1979) for use with adults. With children who are at the stage of concrete operational thought, the therapist will need to translate abstract concepts into concrete understandable ideas. These should be ideas that relate to the child's everyday life. Ronen (1992) has suggested that Beck's term 'automatic thought' be translated into 'doing something without thinking about it'. As in cognitive-behavioural therapy with adults, metaphors can be helpful. 'Would you try to ride a bike with a broken leg? So how can you expect to learn all your French spellings, as depressed as you are?' Other techniques that may be useful in engaging children include cartoons, poetry, role-play, charades, games, puzzles, imagery and art.

Techniques used

Activity scheduling

Depressed children and adolescents tend to be withdrawn and less active. They predict that they will receive no pleasure from activities and that they will be unable to succeed at things that they were able to do before they became depressed. These predictions are usually false, as it is likely that a child will feel less depressed if engaged in an activity that was pleasurable in the past. The child's mind will be occupied with what he or she is doing and this will act as a diversion from automatic thoughts. It is important for the child to realize that feelings are not black or white, 'depressed' or 'not depressed'. At this stage the concept of using a diary that will continue throughout the therapy is introduced. The child is encouraged to rate mood on a scale of one to ten before and after activities. The first week's homework might be to record mood after each activity to see whether the 'hypothesis', that 'I will feel better when engaged in pleasurable activity', is correct.

The next session would then be to help the child to think of pleasurable activities and the homework would be to carry them out and to monitor pleasure on the activity schedule. Beck (1979) describes scheduling mastery in addition to pleasure activities. The child experiences a positive sense of achievement and realizes he or she can accomplish more than predicted. Thus a cognitive restructuring of the child's capabilities occurs. Possible pitfalls are discussed and it is acknowledged that the child may not be able to carry out the tasks because of unforeseen circumstances. The aim is to try to complete every task and not necessarily to succeed.

Affective education

The link between thoughts, feelings and behaviour is of central importance as is the child's understanding of the model. He or she learns that emotions are experienced along a continuum (Stark, 1990). Discussion encourages the child to reveal emotions and to identify situations that precipitate different feelings. The child learns to recognize emotions in others and to recognize the expressions and behaviour associated with those emotions. Stark et al. (1991) have developed a series of games that can be used with younger children. Obviously depression and

sadness form part of affective education. It is also important to understand other negative and positive emotions, for instance anger. This is
helpful for impulsive and conduct-disordered children who tend to
react to any negative emotion aggressively or label any negative emotion
as anger. However, anger is also a common symptom in depressed
youth and can be a difficult symptom to treat (Stark *et al.*, 1991).
Accurately identifying the negative emotion as sadness can help the
child avoid aggressive outbursts, which are unacceptable in school and
to the family, and which serve to alienate significant others, thus making
the child's situation worse.

Problem solving

Problem solving is a useful component of cognitive-behavioural therapy
with depressed youth (Stark *et al.*, 1991). The child is taught to go
through a series of steps when confronted with a problem. It encourages the child to consider alternative solutions and instils a sense of
hope in that there are possibilities that the child has not thought of. If it
helps the child out of a situation it may give a sense of mastery and
control.

(1) Children are taught to identify the problem.
(2) Children are taught to identify their aim.
(3) Alternative solutions are thought of.
(4) The possible outcomes for each solution are considered.
(5) The best solution is chosen and enacted.
(6) The outcome is evaluated.
(7) Self-reinforcement is used if the outcome is positive; if it is negative
    the alternatives are reconsidered.

Problem solving can be used with internalizing and externalizing problems. In the latter case it can be a helpful way of allowing the child to
stop and think before reacting and to consider alternatives. With
depressed children, who tend to react impulsively when angry, it can
work in a similar way. It is also a useful technique for children with
cognitive distortions. The child who thinks in a rigid manner can realize
that there are alternative solutions and the hopeless child can see that
there are options of which he or she has been unaware. Role play is
sometimes used to introduce problem solving, and puzzles can be
helpful tools with younger children.

Self-instruction training

This is a useful approach, first described by Meichenbaum and
Goodman (1971). Kendall and Braswell (1993) outline the use of self-

instruction for impulsive children. They use self-talk as a strategy to guide their thinking and behaviour. It is important that the child should develop his or her own language for this. 'Now what do I want to happen here?' This technique can also be used to provide coping self-statements and positive rewards. 'Brilliant, you did really well.' It is emphasized that it is important that the child should not make negative self-statements, particularly the depressed child who has a continual string of automatic thoughts. Spence (1994) described problem solving using self-talk.

Social skills training

Many depressed children have difficulties with social skills. They are withdrawn and experience relationship difficulties. Techniques used to remedy these problems include teaching the use of verbal and non-verbal communication and assertiveness through modelling and role play.

Monitoring of automatic thoughts

Examples can be given to enable the child to understand the relation-ship between thoughts, feelings and behaviour. For instance:

> 'Suppose you hear a bang in the night, and you think it's a burglar. How do you feel?'
> 'Scared.'
> 'What if you thought that it was a cat knocking over a milk-bottle, how would you feel then?'
> 'Annoyed.'

A depressed child may be unaware of automatic thoughts that he or she is experiencing. It may be very hard to identify them. The therapist can help the child to 'catch' such thoughts. This is best done immediately; in therapy sessions, if affect changes, ask 'what are you thinking now?' If there is a difficulty the child can be asked to imagine a situation in which she or he felt particularly bad, or role-play can be used to conjure up images for the child.

Stark et al. (1991) introduced the idea of children being 'thought detectives' who seek out negative thoughts. A record of automatic thoughts is kept by the child as homework (for which a wrist counter can be a helpful tool). This record is extended to include the feelings associ-ated or caused by the thoughts and the events that preceded them.

A link can be made between the initial event, thoughts, feelings and subsequent behaviour. The child may believe that he or she shouted because his or her brother changed the television channel. The therapist helps the child to realize that the thought 'he always gets his own way;

he doesn't care about me; he shouldn't be allowed to get away with it' made him or her feel angry, and this, rather than the brother's action, caused him or her to shout.

McAdam and Gilbert (1985) noted that the act of writing down thoughts and fears gives stability and structure to adolescents. They can thus feel in control and take responsibility for their thoughts and fears, even when the therapist is not there. The self-control techniques described by Kanfer (1975), self-monitoring, self-evaluation and self-reinforcement can be usefully applied. Self-reinforcement involves the child self-rewarding target behaviour such as monitoring automatic thoughts. The rewards can be food or drink, positive self-statements, people, objects or activities. It is important that they are immediate; this procedure can be started in the clinic and practised as homework.

Challenging automatic thoughts

The therapist asks, and then encourages the child to ask, whether there is any other explanation for a negative thought that occurs. The thought will be totally believed by the child but asking this question introduces the idea that it may be false. The evidence is examined, possibly using the 'thought detective' approach: 'what is the evidence for this thought?' The evidence for and against can be tabulated. The child's belief in the thought, before and after the evidence is examined and included in the table on a scale of one to ten. It is important to establish that a decline of belief from 10 to say 8 is a success for the child.

A simple Likert scale is useful for countering dichotomous thinking (Wilkes et al., 1988). If the child says that everything is awful at home, ask what is the worst the situation at home could possibly be, and what the best situation would be. Then ask how the past week has been. It is likely that the mark will not be placed at the extremely awful end and that the patient will therefore be able to see that things are not quite as bad as first thought.

Other techniques include asking the child what she or he would say to a friend in the same situation. The depressed child tends to be kinder to a friend and to be more exacting towards him or herself. If he or she applies this 'double standard', the 'evidence' for it can be explored. Role reversal is a useful tool. One child believed she had been rejected by a friend who did not come over as promised to play. When she was placed in her friend's shoes she was able to see that her granny had come unexpectedly and that this meant she could not play. She had been aware of this before, but had disqualified the evidence for it and had generalized a belief in total rejection.

It may be that the automatic thought is true. In this case the technique of 'inference chaining' can be used. Here the meaning of a thought is sought.

'Your friend didn't come because she doesn't like you – what if this were true?'
'No one else will like me and I won't have any friends.'
'What if that were true?'
'I'd be all alone.'
'What if that were true?'
'I'd be a worthless person.'

The therapist can encourage the child to challenge these other automatic thoughts.

Homework might involve monitoring automatic thoughts and associated feelings and then challenging them. Cue cards strategically placed around the house or in a school bag, or an alarm watch that goes off at intervals, can be used to remind the child to complete homework assignments and to make positive self-statements.

Modifying basic assumptions

In the above example, if inference chaining was continued the child might say: 'To be a worthwhile person, I must be liked by all people at all times.' This is a schema that is commonly held by depressed children. As therapy progresses, the child's unique schemata are examined. They can be very resistant to change as they are fundamental to the child's self-concept. Change, however, can be easier in children and adolescents than in adults whose schemata are usually more rigidly held. The child, who has been unaware of a basic assumption, may see that it is ludicrous once verbalized. In therapy a link is established between the basic assumption and the young person's thoughts, mood, and behaviour. Changes to these assumptions cannot be imposed. The best evidence against them is provided by the patient (Beck, 1979) so the therapist must avoid giving a 'lesson' but should introduce ideas in a tentative, questioning way. Here experiments, often as homework, are used to try out new schemata. Once the young person has begun to see the negative effect an assumption has upon his or her life, he or she may be ready to adopt a new schema that seems to fit for the child. Adolescents, who have reached formal operational thought, are good at generating alternative hypotheses (McAdam, 1986). They are looking for their own ways of viewing the world and can be more ready than adults to adopt a new schema if they believe that it makes sense for them.

Family intervention and group work

Family intervention

Stark (1990) describes the use of cognitive-behavioural therapy with families. It is important that families understand the rationale behind the therapy, thus enabling them to help the child with homework – particularly the use of self-reinforcement – and to generalize techniques learned in therapy to the world outside.

A specific programme for working with adolescent suicide attempters and their families has been developed: *Successful Negotiation Acting Positively* (SNAP, Rotheram-Borus *et al.*, 1994). SNAP aims to create a positive family atmosphere, teach problem-solving skills and shift understanding of family problems to troublesome situations, rather than difficult individuals. Techniques include the use of a 'feeling thermometer' and tokens given by family members and the therapist to reinforce positive statements and shape appropriate behaviour.

Wilkes *et al.* (1988) created the 'Dyadic Mood Monitor'. This might be filled in independently by an overinvolved parent and child where both believe that neither can be happy if the other is sad. Pointing out occasions when one is enjoying himself or herself and the other is not will help them to see the error of the thought.

Group work

We have developed a cognitive-behavioural therapy group for preadolescent children referred to a child psychiatric service. Children with a variety of diagnoses have been accepted into the group. This ensures adequate numbers of referrals. Vostanis *et al.* (1994) noted that there may be insufficient depressed children or adolescents to set up a group within a clinical setting. Moreover, Fine *et al.* (1989) found that it can be difficult to motivate depressed children to attend a group and that such a group may be very dull and slow moving. They suggest a mixed diagnostic group may be preferable. Children with diagnosis of depression, anxiety and conduct disorder (including mixed disorder of conduct and emotions) have joined the group. We have found that children from each diagnostic category have shown improvement. Exclusion criteria are psychosis and severe learning difficulties.

The group runs for 10 one-hour sessions at weekly intervals, with six children aged 8–12 years, and two therapists. The sessions are structured and have an agenda. The group is designed as a series of games culminating in the creation of a board game. Cognitive-behavioural therapy ideas are introduced and are developed through these games, each of which is represented by a different colour on the board. Incorporating fun into the therapy makes it acceptable to this age group. The games that we have adapted are:

• *Emotional card games* (red) – adapted from 'affective education' (Stark *et al.*, 1991). These games are introduced in the first session and repeated and developed. The group brainstorms emotions which are then shown to be on a continuum. Emotion cards are passed round the group, discussed and enacted, the aim being to enable children to recognize and differentiate, for instance, sadness from anger in themselves and others. Links are made between events, thoughts, feelings and behaviour. Photographs of the children and charades are used. Children are asked question such as:

'what might a person feeling sad be doing?'
'how might he be looking?'
'what might she be thinking?'
'how might he be behaving?'
'what were you doing the last time you felt this?'
'what were you thinking?'

- *Positive statements and reinforcement* (dark blue) – children are encouraged, through the use of a ball game, to make and accept positive statements about themselves and others. This is an opening game for each session.
- *Problem solving* (light blue) – the problem-solving technique is taught using cards describing imaginary situations; for example 'You are in the school dinner queue, someone runs past and knocks your dinner out of your hand. What do you do?' 'Your best friend is going to the cinema and asks someone else to go with them. What do you do?' 'You answer a question in class and get it wrong, everyone laughs at you. What do you do?' Children are given problem-solving sheets to use between sessions and these are discussed within the group. Affect is incorporated to identify the links between thoughts, feelings and behaviour.
- *Problem-solving charades* (yellow) – children enact problematic situations taken from the cards and homework using the problem-solving technique. Photographs are taken and used in the board game.
- *Expert adviser* (green) – adapted from Wragg (1990). Children are asked to imagine their own 'expert adviser' who gives good advice and talks sense. Images are produced and are taken away between sessions and a game piece is made with which to play the board game. This enables children to engage in the abstract concept of monitoring and challenging automatic thoughts and helps them to learn self-control. Children are encouraged to use their 'expert' in problem-solving. The 'expert adviser' is also incorporated into the charades. Children take on the roles of being each other's 'expert' and act as their own 'expert' in problems given as homework. General group processes are used alongside cognitive-behavioural therapy as an enjoyable way of engaging children in a cognitive-behavioural therapy group. This observation is supported by the fact that there is typically a high attendance and no dropouts.

Children are evaluated at pre- and post-group stages and at 3 months. Results have been promising so far and further research is intended.

Conclusion

There is evidence to show that the links between thought, affect and behaviour described by Beck in adults are present in children and adolescents. Many of the automatic thoughts, cognitive errors and maladaptive schemata are also found in depressed youth.

Cognitive-behavioural therapy has been shown to be a successful treatment for depressed adults. There has recently been growing interest in its use with depressed children and adolescents. Various techniques drawn from cognitive and behavioural therapy can be applied when working with depressed young people. The balance of cognitive and behavioural techniques chosen will depend upon the developmental level of the child or adolescent, the symptomatology and the stage of treatment. The techniques and structure of this approach provide an active, theoretically based treatment that enables the depressed young person to engage.

References

Abramson L, Seligman M, Teasdale J (1978) Learned helplessness in humans: critique and reformulation. Journal of Abnormal Psychology 87: 49–74.

Beck AT (1963) Thinking and depression: 1, idiosyncratic content and cognitive distortions. Archives of General Psychiatry 9: 324–33.

Beck AT (1979) Cognitive Therapy of Depression. New York: The Guilford Press.

Clarke GE, Hawkins W, Murphy M, Sheeber LB, Lewinsohn PM, Seeley JR (1995) Targeted prevention of unipolar depressive disorder in an at-risk sample of high school adolescents: a randomised trial of group cognitive intervention. Journal of the American Academy of Child and Adolescent Psychiatry 34(3): 312–21.

Curry JF, Craighead WE (1990) Attributional style in clinically depressed and conduct disordered adolescents. Journal of Consulting and Clinical Psychology 58: 109–16.

Durlak JA, Fuhrman T, Lampman C (1991) Effectiveness of cognitive-behavior therapy for maladapting children: a meta-analysis. Psychological Bulletin 110(2): 204–14.

Ellis A (1962) Reason and Emotion in Psychotherapy. New York: Lyle Stuart.

Fine S, Gilbert M, Schmidt L, Haley G, Maxwell A, Forth A (1989) Short-term group therapy with depressed adolescent outpatients. Canadian Journal of Psychiatry 34(2): 97–102.

Fine S, Forth A, Gilbert M, Haley G (1991) Group therapy for adolescent depressive disorder: a comparison of social skills training and therapeutic support. Journal of the American Academy of Child and Adolescent Psychiatry 30 (1) 79–85.

Haley G, Fine S, Marriage K, Moretti M, Freeman R (1985) Cognitive bias and depression in psychiatrically disturbed children and adolescents. Journal of Consulting and Clinical Psychology 53: 535–7.

Harrington RC, Fudge H, Rutter M, Pickles A, Hill J (1991) Adult outcomes of child and adolescent depression: II. Risk for antisocial disorders. Journal of the American Academy of Child and Adolescent Psychiatry 30: 434–9.

Harrington R (1992) Annotation: the natural history and treatment of child and adolescent affective disorders. Journal of Child Psychology and Psychiatry 33(8): 1287–302.

Kanfer FH (1975) Self-management methods. In Kanfer FH, Goldstein AP (Eds) Helping People Change. New York: Pergamon Press.

Kaslow NJ, Rehm LP, Siegel AW (1984) Social and cognitive correlates of depression in children. Journal of Abnormal Child Psychology 12(4): 605–20.

Kaslow NJ, Rehm LP, Pollack SL, Siegel AW (1988) Attributional style and self-control behaviour in depressed and nondepressed children and their parents. Journal of Abnormal Child Psychology 16: 163–75.

Kazdin AE (1989) Developmental differences in depression. In Lahey BB, Kazdin AE (Eds) Advances in Clinical Child Psychology 12. New York: Plenum Press.

Kempton T, Hasselt VB, Bukstein OG, Null JA (1994) Cognitive distortions and psychiatric diagnosis in dually diagnosed adolescents. Journal of the American Academy of Child and Adolescent Psychiatry 33(2) 217–22.

Kendall PC (1991) Guiding theory for treating children and adolescents. In Kendall PC (Ed) (1991) Child and Adolescent Therapy: Cognitive-behavioral Procedures. New York: Guilford Press.

Kendall PC (1993) Cognitive-behavioural therapy with youth: guiding theory, current status, and emerging developments. Journal of Consulting and Clinical Psychology 64(2) 235–47.

Kendall PC, Stark KD, Adam T (1990) Cognitive deficit or cognitive distortion in childhood depression. Journal of Abnormal Child Psychology 18: 255–70.

Kendall PC, Braswell L (1993) Cognitive-behavioral therapy for impulsive children (second edition). New York: Guilford Press.

Kovacs M, Rush AJ, Beck AT, Hollow SD (1981) Depressed outpatients treated with cognitive therapy or pharmacotherapy. Archives of General Psychiatry 38: 33–9.

Lewinsohn PM, Clarke GN, Hops H, Andrews J (1990) Cognitive-behavioural treatment for depressed adolescents. Behaviour Therapy 21: 385–401.

McAdam EK (1986) Cognitive behaviour therapy and its application with adolescents. Journal of Adolescence 9: 1–15.

McAdam EK, Gilbert P (1985) Cognitive behavioural therapy as a psychotherapy for mood disturbance in child, adolescent and family psychiatry. Newsletter of the Association of Child and Adolescent Psychiatry 7: 19–27.

Meichenbaum D (1977) Cognitive behaviour modification: an integrative approach. New York: Plenum Press.

Meichenbaum D, Goodman J (1971) Training impulsive children to talk to themselves: a means of developing self-control. Journal of Abnormal Child Psychology 77: 115–26.

Mullins LL, Siegel LJ, Hodges, K (1985) Cognitive problem-solving and life event correlates of depressive symptoms in children. Journal of Abnormal Child Psychology 13: 305–14.

Piaget J (1977) The Origin of Intelligence in the Child. London: Penguin Books.

Reynolds WM, Coats KI (1986) A comparison of cognitive-behavioral therapy and relaxation training for the treatment of depression in adolescents. Journal of Consulting and Clinical Psychology 54: 653–60.

Ronen T (1992) Cognitive therapy with young children. Child Psychiatry and Human Development 23(1) 19–30.

Rotheram-Borus MJ, Trautman P, Dopkins SC, Shrout P (1990) Cognitive style and pleasant activities among female adolescent suicide attempters. Journal of Consulting and Clinical Psychology 58: 554–61.

Rotheram-Borus MJ, Piacentini J, Miller S, Graae F, Castro-Blanco D (1994) Brief cognitive-behavioral treatment for adolescent suicide attempters and their families. Journal of the American Academy of Child and Adolescent Psychiatry 33(4) 508–17.

Seligman MEP (1975) Helplessness: On Depression Development and Death. San Fransisco: Freeman & Co.

Seligman MEP, Peterson C, Kaslow NJ, Tanenbaum RL, Alloy LB, Abramson LB (1984) Attributional style and depressive symptoms among children. Journal of Abnormal Psychology 93: 235–8.

Spence S (1994) Practitioner review: cognitive therapy with children and adolescents: from theory to practice. Journal of Child Psychology and Psychiatry 35(7): 1191–228.

Stark KD (1990) Childhood depression: school-based intervention. New York: Guilford Press.

Stark KD, Reynolds WM, Kaslow N (1987) A comparison of the relative efficacy of self-control therapy and a behavioural problem-solving therapy for depression in groups. Journal of Abnormal Child Psychology 15: 91–113.

Stark KD, Rouse LW, Livingston R (1991) Treatment of depression during childhood and adolescence: cognitive-behavioral procedures for the individual and family. In Kendall PC (Ed), Child and Adolescent Therapy: Cognitive-Behavioral Procedures. New York: Guilford Press.

Vostanis P, Harrington R (1994) Cognitive-behavioural treatment of depressive disorder in child psychiatric patients: rationale and description of a treatment package. European Child and Adolescent Psychiatry 3(2): 111–23.

Wilkes TCR, Rush AJ (1988) Adaptations of cognitive therapy for depressed adolescents. Journal of the American Academy of Child and Adolescent Psychiatry 27(3): 381–86.

Wragg, J (1990) Talk Sense to Yourself, A Program for Children and Adolescents. Longman: Harlow.

Chapter 6
The Place of Drugs in Treatment

FINN COSGROVE

Introduction

The treatment of young people with drugs finds itself in a kind of Cinderella position in British clinical practice, if not more widely in Europe. Its 'sisters' include, for example, family therapy, interpersonal psychotherapy, cognitive behavioural therapy and social skills training. A child psychiatrist, unlike adult psychiatrists, is also faced with what can be called 'the problem of the product licence'. This refers to the statement that declares that an antidepressant or other psychotropic medication is not recommended for children. Where no age is specified this statement is usually meant to refer to those under 18 years of age. Furthermore, rating scales for the detection of depression in children are not always easily available and tend not to provide a clear differentiation between depressed and non-depressed states. The medical practitioner is therefore faced with: (1) some uncertainty about the diagnosis of depression in the child; (2) a sense of legal threat from the product licence; and (3) a range of professionally acceptable psychological treatments, each of which carries much less medico-legal responsibility for the medical practitioner than the prescribing of antidepressant medication. No wonder, then, that drug treatment is relegated to 'severe cases of depression which have failed to respond to other forms of intervention' (Harrington, 1993). This chapter will argue for a more robust and confident approach to antidepressant psychopharmacology, particularly in the light of the paucity of controlled trials for Cinderella's psychological sisters.

There have been no controlled studies of the treatment of depression in young people using interpersonal psychotherapy or family therapy. One trial has demonstrated that social skills training can be beneficial in adolescent males (not females) (Reed, 1994) but this needs to be replicated. Drugs used for children and adolescents, by contrast, have undergone a number of double-blind, controlled studies – essential for evidence-based medicine. The tricyclic antidepressants have fared badly under this form of testing. The SSRIs (selective serotonin reuptake inhibitors) have yet to be tested for depression in children in double-blind, placebo-controlled trials, although they appear to be useful for obsessive compulsive disorder. The DRAs (dopamine releasing agents) have performed very successfully in very many double-blind, controlled studies, although they have rarely been tested for depression in children and adolescents. It can be seen that, although drugs have been tested more often than alternative therapies, the results have not produced a clear statement for the prescriber.

The child psychiatrist and the product licence

In Britain it is commonly believed that the recommendations in the product licence are legally binding on the medical practitioner. This entirely incorrect professional misconception has a monumental effect upon the drug treatment of depression in young people. In a clear statement of the legal position under the Medicines Act 1968, Dr Ronald Mann writes, in the *Drugs and Therapeutics Bulletin,* that 'Licensing arrangements (the details of the product licence) constrain drug companies but leave doctors free to prescribe unlicensed drugs or to use drugs for unlicensed indications' (Mann, 1992). 'Unlicensed indications' might include, for example, the prescribing of an antidepressant to a child, or prescribing a dose in excess of the recommended daily maximum for any patient (regardless of age). Both these actions are entirely legal and the Medicines Act was, in fact, framed to leave doctors free to use licensed drugs in unlicensed ways as well as to prescribe unlicensed drugs to their patients where clinically necessary (Mann, 1992).

The Act also allows pharmacists to dispense, and nurses to administer, licensed drugs prescribed for unlicensed purposes as well as unlicensed drugs. Consequently, the pharmacist and nurse have no reason to fear legal action when enabling a depressed child to receive an antidepressant prescribed by a child psychiatrist or other registered medical practitioner. The intentions of the British Medicines Act appear to be the same for other European Union countries. In principle, the situation in Germany is comparable (Hopf, 1995). The child psychiatrist is not, in practice, faced with the need to prescribe an unlicensed medicine for the depressed child because all the drugs likely to be considered are licensed – albeit for use in adults. In law, the child psychiatrist (along with other medical colleagues including the child's general practitioner whom the psychiatrist may be advising) is allowed to depart from the prescribing directions given in the product licence. In departing from the recommendation that a particular drug should not be used in young people, the child psychiatrist needs to be aware of the reasonable nature of such a decision. Under the Medicines Act, articles and book chapters advising such usage in children and adolescents must not be published by, or on behalf of, the pharmaceutical industry. This chapter is not linked in any way to any of the drug companies, and will seek to justify the use of antidepressant medication for depressed children and adolescents.

Which neurotransmitter system?

The noradrenergic system

As antidepressants target one or more neurotransmitter chemicals, it is worth considering neurotransmitter systems both in terms of their possible involvement in depression and their level of maturity in the young person. There is evidence that the noradrenergic system does not develop fully, either functionally or anatomically, until early adulthood (Goldman-Rakic et al., 1982; Smolen et al., 1985). Furthermore, in adolescents there is a high level of ketosteroids, which influence the working of the noradrenergic system (Ryan, 1992). It is hardly surprising, therefore, that nortriptyline and desipramine, the pure noradrenergic antidepressants, have consistently failed to demonstrate antidepressant effectiveness greater than placebo (Hazell et al., 1995). Imipramine and amitriptyline have been no more successful, even though they have some serotonergic properties as well. Imipramine and amitriptyline are metabolized in the liver more swiftly in children than in adults. This shifts the mildly serotonergic properties of imipramine and amitriptyline towards the noradrenergic properties of their metabolites (Ryan, 1992). As a consequence, imipramine and amitriptyline act via their metabolites as relatively pure noradrenergic drugs, thereby failing as antidepressants in childhood because of the immaturity of the noradrenergic neurotransmitter system. In view of the failure of many double-blind, placebo-controlled trials of noradrenergic antidepressants in children, and because of the evidence that the young person's noradrenergic system is immature and may not be able to respond to noradrenergic antidepressants as the adult system can, it is argued that attention should be turned to other neurotransmitter systems such as the serotonergic and dopaminergic systems.

The serotonergic system

The pharmaceutical industry has taken the lead in focusing the profession's attention on drugs that target serotonin transmitter functions. This has resulted in the use of selective serotonin reuptake inhibitors

(SSRIs): fluoxetine, paroxetine, sertraline, fluvoxamine and, more recently, citalopram. In adults, these have shown antidepressant benefits equivalent to those of imipramine and other noradrenergic antidepressants but with fewer histaminergic and anticholinergic side-effects and with greater safety in overdose. Little is known about the functional maturity of the serotonergic system in young people but it cannot be assumed that the effectiveness of SSRIs in adults will be automatically repeated in depressed children. There is, nevertheless, evidence that the SSRIs are effective in addressing obsessive compulsive disorder (OCD) in children (Riddle *et al.*, 1992). This may be an indication that SSRIs might not be effective antidepressants in children on the grounds that OCD is a specifically serotonergic dysfunction unlike depression which involves one or more other neurotransmitter systems. To date, no double-blind, placebo-controlled trials have been performed using the SSRIs for depression in children. This may be partly because depression is uncommon in childhood, especially when compared with attention deficit hyperactivity disorder and conduct disorder. Drug companies are also reluctant to become involved in such studies on account of the unlicensed use of the SSRIs in people under 18 years of age. Similarly, clinical researchers, although willing to conduct trials on the older tricyclics (some of which are licensed for enuresis in children), may be reluctant to conduct trials of SSRIs on account of possible difficulty in obtaining approval from the local ethics committee. They should be encouraged by the good side-effect profile in adults and the emerging effectiveness of SSRIs in children with OCD.

The dopaminergic system

Drug manufacturers take the lead in the clinical use of antidepressants. If they decide to pay attention to one neurotransmitter system whilst ignoring another then the medical profession will follow. This occurred when the focus of attention switched from predominantly noradrenergic antidepressants to the SSRIs. Many psychiatrists are enthusiastic to try the latest antidepressant with adults – and with good reason because they are always hoping for a greater benefit:side-effect ratio. There is currently a shift from the early SSRIs to the first SNRI (serotonin and noradrenaline reuptake inhibitor) called venlafaxine. However, the patient population in mind is adult; the doctors visited by sales representatives are psychiatrists who work with adults and general practitioners (the latter thinking in terms of their adult patients) and the new SNRI still focuses on the serotonergic and noradrenergic neurotransmitter systems. So children remain neglected.

There is, however, one neurotransmitter system which will almost certainly never be considered by the pharmaceutical industry for use in adult depression. This is the dopaminergic system. It is believed that dopaminergic medication is so likely to produce psychosis in adults that psychiatrists would not use them and sales would be poor. Furthermore, these medicines (methylphenidate, dexamphetamine and pemoline) are more closely linked to the illicit drug scene than the noradrenergic and serotonergic antidepressants. It is interesting to note that fluoxetine is being used in combination with the illicit drug, ecstasy. Perhaps there are no antidepressants free from the possibility of being abused.

The dopamine neurotransmitter system continues to be well studied because of its involvement in schizophrenia and in attention deficit hyperactivity disorder. Dopaminergic neurones in the ventral segmental area of the midbrain send axons to the limbic system and to the prefrontal cortex. Dopamine release in these areas results in the experience of pleasure, and it is likely that dopamine is involved in depression (Nutt, 1993). Thus dopaminergic medications such as deprenyl (MAOIB), bromocriptine and piribedyl (dopamine agonists) and buproprion (a dopamine reuptake inhibitor) have useful antidepressant effects (Brown *et al.*, 1993). One case study reported that the dopamine releasing agent dexamphetamine, when added to fluoxetine, produced clinical improvement in the adult patient whose depression was resistant to noradrenergics and to fluoxetine alone (Gupta *et al.*, 1992). Furthermore, the effectiveness of electroconvulsive therapy (ECT) is considered to be related to its capacity to increase the availability of dopamine as well as serotonin and noradrenaline.

Agents releasing dopamine from the presynaptic terminal (DRAs or dopamine releasing agents) have been repeatedly shown to be effective in treating children with attention deficit hyperactivity disorder (ADHD). Indeed, in contrast with most psychotropic medicines, the DRAs methylphenidate, dexamphetamine and pemoline are licensed for use with children but not for adults. Methylphenidate has been subjected to more double-blind, placebo-controlled trials than any other psychotropic medication used for children and adolescents. It has shown itself superior to placebo in regard to behavioural problems (aggression, impulsiveness, overactivity) and academic problems (inattention, reading/spelling/arithmetic retardation, poor work output, poor memory). It is difficult to believe that a medicine capable of producing such a wide range of improvements has no effect on depression in a child. Kelly *et al.* (1989) have demonstrated clinically significant improvement in self-esteem in a double-blind study of ADHD children treated with methylphenidate.

In answer to the question 'Which neurotransmitter system?' the child psychiatrist needs to be aware of:

(1) the immaturity of the noradrenergic system and the repeated ineffectiveness of antidepressants targeting this system;
(2) the effectiveness of the SSRIs in childhood OCD and their low side-effect profile even in overdose;
(3) the long-established experience with DRAs licensed for children in a wide range of behavioural and cognitive problems associated with ADHD, where dopamine insufficiency is probable.

Which antidepressant?

Noradrenergic reuptake inhibitors

In a meta-analysis of the effectiveness of tricyclic drugs (which have a predominantly noradrenergic action) Hazell *et al.* (1995) studied 12 placebo-controlled trials in depressed young people ranging from 6–18 years. Their conclusion was that tricyclic antidepressants appear to be no more effective than placebo in the treatment of depression in children and adolescents. The tricyclic drugs studied were: amitriptyline, imipramine, desipramine, nortriptyline and clomipramine. In view of their similar noradrenergic reuptake characteristics, the following tricyclics can reasonably be added to this list: dothepin, doxepin, amoxepine, lofepramine, protriptyline and trimipramine. The mechanisms of action of the tetracylics mianserin and maprotiline are incompletely understood although they are likely to have noradrenergic reuptake properties similar to the tricylics. Mianserin requires monthly full blood counts in order to check for leucopenia, aplastic anemia and agranulocytosis.

A few deaths have occurred in children on imipramine, desipramine and maprotiline. Popper and Elliott (1990) have argued that desipramine induces QT prolongation and that this conduction abnormality is associated with ventricular arrhythmias. One consequence is that children are likely to be subjected to ECGs prior to starting a tri- or tetracyclic antidepressant and whenever dosage increases occur or a steady state is reached. Birmaher and colleagues in Pittsburgh have developed ECG guidelines which they consider would not alarm parents and which include easy access to a cardiologist (Ryan, 1992). The antidepressant is to be reduced or stopped if the PR interval is greater than 0.18–0.2 seconds or if the QRS complex is greater than 0.48 seconds or widens more than 50% over the baseline, or if the corrected QT interval is greater than 0.48 seconds, or if the resting heart rate or blood pressure are higher than certain levels. This does seem very complicated and even if it does not alarm parents it will surely worry most child psychiatrists. In view of the failure to demonstrate antidepressant efficacy in children, and given the biological explanations put forward, is it really ever necessary to prescribe cyclic antidepressants to children? When SSRIs have not been shown to be ineffective, and when DRAs are licensed for use in children, should not a serotonergic or dopaminergic psychotropic medicine be used, thus avoiding all the ECG monitoring necessary for the noradrenergic antidepressants? It is considered that a child psychiatrist would be in a weak position in court following the death of a child taking a tricyclic or tetracyclic antidepressant. Not only would it be difficult to demonstrate with certainty that the child was depressed prior to treatment but the decision to use a noradrenergic drug in the light of their demonstrated ineffectiveness and their potentially lethal side-effect profile would find little or no support from professional peers. Furthermore, barristers would surely find loopholes in the ECG monitoring and interpretation because of the complexity involved. There would be no legal protection provided by the drug companies because neither the tricyclics nor maprotiline and mianserin are licensed to be used as antidepressants in children and persons under the age of 18 years.

Serotonergic reuptake inhibitors

These are either selective serotonin reuptake inhibitors or serotonin and noradrenaline reuptake inhibitors of which venlafaxine is the first. However, because of its noradrenergic properties, this SNRI would come under the same criticism as the tricyclic antidepressants and would not be recommended for use in young people. There are six SSRIs at the present time: fluoxetine, fluvoxamine, paroxetine, sertraline, nefazodone and citalopram. Although none of these is licensed for children, the medical practitioner in the UK and probably in Europe may legally prescribe them for patients under the age of 18. Unlike the noradrenergics, the SSRIs have shown themselves to be safe in overdosage in adults. This should encourage the child psychiatrist to prescribe them for children particularly when they have been used in young people with OCD and are recommended for bulimic patients who may well be below the age of 18.

Dosage recommendations for adults need not straitjacket prescribing decisions for young people. There is no reason why the initial dose should not be the lowest daily dose recommended in the licence, but given once every three to four days. This can be increased periodically to one day in every two or three before reaching the daily adult dose. This allows the SSRI to be used in prepubertal children and gives the mother and clinician more time to monitor progress and side-effects. The study dosage in a double-blind, crossover trial of fluoxetine in children and adolescents with OCD was 20 mg daily (Riddle *et al.*, 1992). This should encourage clinicians in prescribing fluoxetine for young children. Out of the 14 children in this study, only one child was withdrawn because of side-effects. Otherwise side-effects were generally well tolerated. Fluoxetine is not associated with suicidal acts or ideation any more than placebo or tricyclic antidepressants (Beasley *et al.*, 1991). In this meta-analysis of over 3,000 patients, suicidal ideation actually improved significantly more than with placebo ($p < 0.001$). The SSRIs have little or no effect on cholinergic, histaminergic or noradrenergic receptors, so drowsiness, somnolence, dry mouth and postural hypotension are not usually associated with these drugs when compared with the tricyclics. Nausea, appetite reduction, fatigue and wakefulness can occur but are usually transient. Administering the medication with food can help alleviate nausea. It is not always obvious whether the child is more comfortable when the dosage is given at the beginning of the day or towards the evening, so a 'trial and error' approach is justified.

Exceeding the daily recommended dosage is acceptable as long as any increases in the dose are carried out incrementally, slowly, and in a context where the parent or young person has easy access to the clinician. It is not obvious or, indeed, logical to conclude that a universally recommended dose (such as 20 mg daily for fluoxetine) will have the optimum antidepressant effect on each and every child and adolescent. Bearing in mind their safety in overdose, and that for fluoxetine a daily dose of 60 mg is recommended for bulimia (compared with 20 mg daily for depression), it is reasonable to be willing to move beyond the maximum dosage recommendations in the licence in some young people. The first step beyond the licensed recommended dose can be to give a larger than 'maximum' dose on alternate days and observe, titrating dosage against clinical benefits and side-effects. It is a pity to stay at a lower dose when testing a higher one might give satisfaction to patient, parents and prescriber. Telemedicine is an important part of prescribing for children so that contact on the phone outside booked appointments reassures both clinician and parents. Short appointments of, say, 15 minute duration can allow many children to be seen as outpatients.

There is no need to list the dosage regimes recommended by the licences for these six SSRIs because they are found in the MIMS or the BNF (in Britain) and equivalent doctors' drug handbooks in other countries. It is worth possessing a copy of the product monograph as well as the brief data sheet. Remember that all drug companies have medical information services and a phone call for any query is invariably informative and helpful. (The relevant telephone numbers are found at the back of MIMS and BNF.) They will send the product monograph, which provides information about the drug in a user-friendly way. The medical information staff will check through their database and provide articles or references on any aspect of their products.

The place of SSRIs in the treatment of depression in children has not been established by double-blind, placebo-controlled trials. Such studies are very likely to be forthcoming as clinical researchers become increasingly disillusioned with the noradrenergic antidepressants. In the meanwhile, there appears to be no contraindication to their use for depression in children. However, if the depression does not respond to the SSRIs, then the child psychiatrist's attention should be drawn to the patient's dopaminergic system.

Dopamine releasing agents

We have already seen that dopamine can be related to depression, and that a number of drugs that increase dopaminergic transmission have antidepressant properties. The problem facing the child psychiatrist is that the drug companies do not market the dopamine releasing agents (DRAs – methylphenidate, dexamphetamine and pemoline) for depression even in adults. They do provide them for children with ADHD, which is a relatively common condition. There is clinical evidence that children with ADHD have features of depression such as low self-esteem, excessive crying, and chronic unhappiness. As depression is extremely difficult to diagnose in children it may well be that many children with ADHD are also clinically depressed. Certainly the response to the DRAs (which are reported to be effective in 70–80% of ADHD sufferers) shows a marked improvement in happiness and self-confidence. As DRAs improve depressive features in children with ADHD, it may be that they will be effective for depressed children without ADHD, particularly if the SSRIs have been unhelpful. Of course, it may be that the depressed child has some mild, unrecognized features of ADHD.

The DRAs are licensed for use in children manifesting problems, and this contrasts with SSRIs and tricylics which are not. Thus, sharing responsibility with the manufacturer, the child psychiatrist can feel encouraged to prescribe a DRA even if there is uncertainty about a formal diagnosis of depression but where excessive unhappiness and crying with low self-esteem are present. There is so much experience with the DRAs in children that the prescriber is moving along a well-worn path. It was estimated that, in the USA alone, 600,000 children per year were receiving methylphenidate (Safer and Krager, 1983). This is between 1–2% of the school age population and should be compared to the prevalence of ADHD of 3–5%. In a Medline search of Ritalin, 48 double-blind, placebo-controlled trials were found that demonstrated the effectiveness of this DRA over placebo. Most antidepressants in use with adults have not been subjected to so much vigorous testing.

Methylphenidate is not an amphetamine but has a piperidine molecule. The onset of action of both methylphenidate and dexamphetamine occurs one hour after ingestion and behavioural improvements last for 3–5 hours. The required dose might sometimes be as frequent as five times per day. The manufacturers of pemoline recommend a once daily dose but many mothers and some clinicians believe that better thera-peutic efficacy occurs with a dose frequency similar to methylphenidate and dexamphetamine. The DRAs do tend to produce a fall in appetite which may result in a drop in weight. This change in appetite is usually transient. Some children feel better about themselves after losing some weight, however, so this is not always counterproductive. Wakefulness may be a side-effect of the DRAs but, sometimes, a low dosage in the evening can settle the child earlier. Headaches, abdominal pain (due to drug precipitated constipation) and tics can occur. There is no evidence that DRAs produce a shorter adult height if they are stopped before the epiphysial closure (Klein *et al* 1988).

Dosage should start with half a tablet to be taken twice daily for about a week. This means 5 mg bd for methylphenidate (10 mg), 2.5 mg bd for dexamphetamine (5 mg) and 10 mg for pemoline (20 mg). Pemoline comes as Volital (20 mg) and Cylert (37.5 mg) and without doubt the 20 mg tablet is easier to manage. Dosages can then be raised at intervals of about one week by the equivalent of a full tablet in divided doses through the day. The maximum recommended doses are what they say – 'recommended' and nothing else. As discussed in the section on the product licence, the clinical needs of the patient may require incremental increases which take the daily dose above the manufac-turer's maximum in the licence. It is perfectly legal to exceed the maximum dose in these circumstances and this should be done with no hesitation if clinically necessary.

The duration of DRA treatment, once a stable, optimum dose has been found, is controversial. Psychiatrists who treat adults have a similar problem with patients who do well on other antidepressants. The devel-oping consensus is to err on the side of continued treatment rather than risk deterioration in the patient's health. This is probably also the correct principle in young people. The DRAs can be stopped over a couple of days for a one-week period during term time and/or the long summer holiday. If depression recurs then administration of DRA should be continued immediately.

Reversible inhibitor of monoamine oxidase A

If specific targeting of both the serotonergic and dopaminergic systems is unsuccessful, it may well be worth trying moclobemide which is a reversible inhibitor of monoamine oxidase A. This does not require any dietary restrictions except avoidance of large amounts of mature cheese, fermented soya bean products and yeast extracts, which are not part of a sensible, ordinary diet in any case. Exactly the same principle should be applied to moclobemide as to any of the SSRIs or DRAs. Start with a dose lower than the recommended starting dose for adults and gently raise it according to clinical response and side-effects (if any).

Moclobemide has been used effectively in children with ADHD and may have a place for young people with depression.

Concluding comments

Parents are not as fearful of drugs prescribed for behavioural and emotional disorders, nor as antagonistic to them, as is sometimes thought. They have often experienced some form of ineffective counselling or family therapy and are still left with a troubled child. As long as they understand that they can hear the prescriber's voice on the telephone, or can arrange short appointments within a few days of calling for help, they are often willing to try a tablet for their child's psychosocial problems, including depression. If the child psychiatrist is confident and makes sensible comments about starting at a very low dosage and raising it up slowly, parents will be encouraged to cooperate and to ensure that the tablets are given at the right time. Frequent but short outpatient appointments are appreciated by the child and parents. They also demonstrate that the prescriber is behaving in a responsible and peer approved manner.

The child psychiatrist should be sufficiently aware of the law relating to the product licence (in the UK this is the Medicines Act 1968). Information about this may be found in Mann (1992) which can be obtained through libraries. The realization that licensing arrangements are in force to control the manufacturer and the distributors but not the registered medical practitioner allows the doctor to benefit from the information on the data sheet without being bound by it to the disadvantage of the young patient.

Never forget that drug companies are mines of information on their own products and that their medical information staff are always of great assistance to the prescriber, especially as they can use their databases built up over years and across many countries. They are not allowed to say anything positive about the use of their antidepressant outside the licence but they would be willing to send articles on unlicensed usage to you (including use with children). Do not forget to ask for the product monograph.

Drug treatment has a place in the management of depressed children. It does not exclude psychosocial treatment modalities taking place simultaneously. Whilst the noradrenergic tricyclic and tetracyclic antidepressants cannot be recommended for children (not even for enuresis now that desmopressin is available, effective and safe), the SSRIs show promise as evidenced by childhood OCD treatment. The DRAs are also so well known and so frequently used in ADHD that prescribing them for depression in childhood should not present a problem to the child psychiatrist, especially as they are licensed for use in children.

References

Beasley CM Jr, Dornseif BE, Bosomworth JC, Sayler ME, Rampey AH Jr, Heiligenstein JH, Thompson VL, Murphy DJ, Masica DN (1991) Fluoxetine and suicide: a meta-analysis of controlled trials of treatment for depression. British Medical Journal 303(6804): 685–92.

Brown AS, Gershon S (1993) Dopamine and depression. Journal of Neural Transmission 91: 75–109.

Goldman-Rakic P, Brown PM (1982) Postnatal development of monoamine content and synthesis in the cerebral cortex of rhesus monkeys. Developmental Brain Research 4: 339–49.

Gupta S, Ghaly N, Dewan M (1992) Augmenting fluoxetine with dextroamphetamine to treat refractory depression. Hospital and Community Psychiatry 43 (3): 281–3.

Harrington R (1993) Depressive Disorder in Childhood and Adolescence (see page 187). Chichester: John Wiley.

Hazell P, O'Connell D, Heathcote D, Robertson J, Henry D (1995) Efficacy of tricyclic drugs in treating child and adolescent depression: a meta-analysis. British Medical Journal 310: 897–901.

Hopf G (1995) Personal communication.

Kelly PC, Cohen ML, Walker WO, Caskey OL, Atkinson AW (1989) Self-esteem in children medically managed for attention deficit disorder. Pediatrics 83(2): 211–17.

Klein RG, Landa B, Mattes JA, Klein DF (1988) Methylphenidate and growth in hyperactive children. A controlled withdrawal study. Archives of General Psychiatry 45(12): 1127–30.

Mann R (1992) Prescribing unlicensed drugs or using drugs for unlicensed indications. Drug and Therapeutic Bulletin 30(25): 97–9

Nutt D (1993) Neurochemistry and Neuropharmacology. In Morgan G, Butler S (Eds) Basic Neurosciences. Gaskell, London.

Riddle MA, Scahill L, King RA, Hardin MT, Anderson GM, Ort SI, Smith JC, Leckman JF, Cohen DJ (1992) Double-blind, crossover trial of fluoxetine and placebo in children and adolescents with obsessive-compulsive disorder. Journal of the American Academy of Child and Adolescent Psychiatry 31(6): 1062–9.

Popper CW, Elliott GR (1990) Sudden death and tricyclic antidepressants: clinical considerations for children. Journal of Child and Adolescent Psychopharmacology 1: 125–32.

Reed MK (1994) Social skills training to reduce depression in adolescents. Adolescence 29(114): 293–302.

Ryan ND (1992) The pharmacologic treatment of child and adolescent depression. Psychiatric Clinics of North America 15(1): 29–40).

Safer DJ, Krager JM (1983) Trends in medication treatment of hyperactive school children. Clinical Pediatrics 22: 500–4.

Smolen AJ, Beaston-Wimmer P, Wright LL et al (1985) Neurotransmitter synthesis, storage and turnover in neonatally deafferented sympathetic neurons. Developmental Brain Research 23: 211–18.

Chapter 7
The Hidden Factor: an Educational Perspective of Depression in Learning

MURIEL BARRETT AND JUDITH WATERFIELD

Introduction

The term 'depression' can be used to describe a state of mind that is brief in duration – a transitory state, such as feeling 'low' – or a potentially long-term state of clinical depression. Salzberger-Wittenburg (1970) refers to the word 'depression' as an 'umbrella' term that covers a variety of painful states, from a 'passing mood of being down in the dumps to a more or less permanent state of misery'. This correlates with our notion of a depressive continuum.

Our main focus is on learning, and how the 'hidden' factor, depression, affects the cognitive or social skills of children and young people. Depression frequently remains hidden in school, either because we, as adults, fail to recognize that certain behaviours, or changed patterns of learning, could be equated with such a condition or because children or young people are too successful at resisting acknowledgement of their depression.

From our experience as mainstream teachers and educational therapists, we believe that some children enter school burdened by depressive feelings from early childhood. As adults we seem unwilling to think that a child's behaviour may be an indication of depression; it is as though we cannot bear to think that those for who we are responsible can be more than just unhappy. Yet, at the time of writing, we have noticed that information on this subject is readily available to the public; in one instance in a popular magazine *Prima* (1995). This publication featured an article, entitled 'So Young and So Sad', which stated that, 'Depression is now a common problem in young children. Look out for the telltale signs in your child. It shouldn't be left untreated.' The readers are referred to Young Minds, a professional organization that produced several pamphlets to alert parents to the symptoms of undue distress in children. Two national daily newspapers also featured articles noting the serious increase in children's and adolescents' mental health problems, including depression. In the *Independent* (1995), Peter Wilson the Director of Young Minds, suggests that parents 'might not be sure how to understand it, whether to be embarrassed or ashamed about it, or indeed know if there's anything that can be done.' In the *Daily Telegraph,* Ferriman (1995) examines the increase in young people's health problems, including suicide.

Defining and differentiating adult and childhood depression

In 1966, Rie commented on the difficulty of defining depression, because its popular concept is 'apparently conducive to semantic complacency, and to a subsequent uncritical application of the term'. He considered the differing psychoanalytical viewpoints of numerous authors, who debated whether there was a need to differentiate between adult and childhood depression. The psychoanalytic stance taken by Rie, and indeed earlier by Freud (1917), failed to recognize childhood depression as a separate syndrome, believing that children lacked the ego-structure necessary to be depressed. It has also been argued that children's symptoms of depression were transitory and therefore could not be considered as a separate syndrome, a viewpoint now refuted.

Twenty years later the work of Stevenson and Romney (1984) noted that: '... although childhood depression exists as a clinical entity it manifests itself in a different form from adult depression, e.g. as a conduct disorder, hyperactivity, somatic symptoms, school phobia, learning disability etc.'

There are a multiplicity of behaviours that are now recognized as part of childhood depression, and there is a better understanding of this experience. Sometimes a child's sadness can be misinterpreted as depression, a distinction made by Higgins (1992) with whom we agree on this point. He considers depression from an interactional point of view.

> The reasons for children's depression are often as obscure to them as to those looking on from outside, trying to understand them. In this respect depression, can antagonise all parties, depressed and undepressed alike.

Received, owned and interactive depressive states of mind

We suggest that, at any juncture on a depressive continuum, be it transitory or long term, there are three concepts that have helped us to understand this upset state of mind.

'Received' depression

In this form we believe depression is received by a child from a significant adult, such as an attachment figure (Bowlby, 1969). The adult
cannot tolerate his or her own depressed feelings (for numerous
reasons) and thus projects them onto a child. Barrett and Trevitt (1991)
suggest that some children 'become sad or depressed as a result of their
parents' past unresolved mourning or current reaction to loss'.

'Owned' depression

Our second concept is a state of mind that has been internalized: it has
become 'owned' by a child. An experience has led the child to believe
that she or he is in some way responsible for one or more traumatic
events. Such children rarely have long-term access to a trusted, emotionally available, attachment figure (Bowlby, 1969) and this results in
damaged attachment patterns, in faulty mourning processes relating to
loss, or to particular circumstances that have led to some type of abuse.
Any of these factors could lead to depression. The term 'owned' depression can also convey the sense of being introjected. Examples of this are
given by Deri (1984). She discusses mothers whose behaviour is intru-
sive and narcissistic, thus reflecting 'a false adoration and an unreal
image' which is introjected by the child, who, when seeking this image
in others later in life, may find that 'a deep, hidden depression may be
[his or her] only authentic experience'. Deri calls the more passive children 'avid introjectors'.

'Interactive' depression

We suggest that received and owned depression may become part of an
interaction. The volume of research on depressed mothers, notably by
Murray (1988), Murray and Trevarthen (1986) and Cohen (1991), has
led to discussions about the long-term effects of this maternal behaviour
on the behaviour of the infants who have been its recipients. In a series
of videos, Murray demonstrates that depressed mothers who have
shown a deficit in maternal communication are less able to focus on
their infants and are critical of their behaviour during a shared task. The
infants cope by becoming easily distracted, turning away, being unable
to sustain interaction and showing less interest in learning. Early and
later learning skills are usually affected, in that the infants have been
inhibited from exploring their environment and other people, thus
making them believe that the world is a dangerous place. (A minority
take recourse in intellectual skills which they pursue to the exclusion of
developing relationships.) If there is a combination of maternal personality disorder and depression, the received experience of the infant is

significantly more damaging. If neither mother nor infant can meet one another's needs there seems a likelihood that interactive depression will be present.

Family attachments

Goodyer (1990) considers the dynamics of dysfunctional families and suggests that, if there is an ongoing disruption of competent parenting, any resultant attentional difficulties manifested by the infant may have implications for school achievement. (We suggest that this would be particularly relevant for children who experience repeated disruption in schools, such as numerous teachers, temporary teachers, or supply teachers.)

Parents who are burdened from their own childhood experience of unresolved loss, abuse or rejection, and who are feeling unloved, are unlikely to be able to care for a baby they felt they wanted and needed. Their mistaken belief that the baby will magically love them is short-lived when the baby makes the very demands for loving care that they themselves have lacked. If partnerships are unsatisfactory, extended family interest or support is lacking, and inadequate environments are added to this situation, mothers, or other attachment figures, may remain in long-term depressive states.

The contribution made to child depression by dysfunctional families, including depressed mothers, is also considered by Wolkind (1984), Snyder and Huntley (1990) and Cohen (1991). Morgan (1994) also takes environmental factors into account. Bowlby's work on attachment and loss (1969, 1973, 1980, 1982) explores and contrasts the behaviour of children who are secure in their relationships with a significant adult, with those who have formed anxious attachments with such a figure. One sentence from a later work summarizes the feelings of most children and their families: 'If all goes well there is joy and a sense of security, if it is threatened there is jealousy and anger, if broken there is grief and depression' (Bowlby, 1988).

Children who are members of a secure family attachment system begin learning by interactions and exploratory play and therefore enter school ready to learn more, with an expectation that teachers will care and meet their cognitive and social needs. They have received positive messages from the time of birth. These messages are gradually internalized and are reflected back to a trusted adult, thus establishing a reciprocated interactive learning process. At a time of separation the secure child can express sadness and anger, and will sometimes slow down in school learning. At a time of actual loss, such as the death of a cherished relation, such a child manages a mourning process and, when feelings relating to such an event become less intense, but subsequent events evoke a memory of the lost figure, secure children internalize a 'good' memory of their relationship with that figure. The messages that such a child has received from surviving family members will have been true: that a parent or sibling has died or been killed, or will not return for whatever reason. This provides a basis of reality on which a child can rebuild his self-worth, and which will enable the child to return to school learning.

Children who have experienced a less secure relationship, and have formed an anxious attachment to a figure of significance, may cling to, or reject, that figure. Following a separation, anxious children are frequently forced to internalize a loss in a distorted form in order to make it more acceptable to the adults caring for them (Bowlby, 1979). The adults may deny the reality of the circumstances of a death so that the child's process of mourning is delayed or never completed. The messages the child has received from this untruthful source are false, the loss remains a mystery, and feelings of 'owned' depression may begin, sometimes leading to the child thinking that it must be his or her fault. Any memory of the 'lost' person becomes too painful to bear and can result in learning impairment and social impairment. One inhibiting factor related to learning is noted by Law (1996) who comments on the poor temporal sense of a five year old who could not learn to read because he could not understand the death of his sister shortly before his own birth.

How do children and young people manage their depressive feelings?

Osmond (1993) feels that 'There is now an acceptance that depression does occur in childhood and that untreated it may result in life-threatening self-destructive behaviour.' The latter part of this opinion is confirmed by the experience of one of the authors (JW) when working with an art therapist in an adolescent unit (Waterfield and Brown, 1996). It was found that some adolescent depression manifested itself in uncontrollable outbursts of anger. When reintrojected, these resulted in several forms of self-harm. Such behaviour is not necessarily limited to young people. Kendall Johnson (1989) examines the cause and effect of trauma in the lives of younger children. He suggests that, in the United States, at the time of writing, children as young as ten very often 'completed suicides' when they suffered the loss of a parent or were learning-disabled. He states that either factor will 'diminish a child's self-esteem'. Amongst other behaviours this author linked with suicides were adolescents who acted out, abused alcohol or drugs, displayed violent behaviour, turned to petty crime, or ran away, any of which he regards as providing short-term relief from coping with depressive feelings. Longer-term relief is managed by adopting psychosomatic symptoms, absolute denial by the adoption of a 'false self' (Winnicott, 1965), or, as in the example of Mary below, silence about a 'taboo' subject.

Mary

Mary, aged 12, had been attending an outpatient clinic for headaches for almost a year. This coincided with her transition to a large comprehensive school. She was supported by parents who accepted the average level of her achievements in school. Her teachers liked her; she was 'never any trouble'. The gradual deterioration in her learning and subsequent headaches from her eleventh birthday were perplexing. The school referred the family to an educational therapist. During the interview it emerged that Mary's elder sister, Margaret, had suffered from headaches and died in her thirteenth year from a brain tumour. Both parents became very upset in recalling this tragic loss. It transpired that they had never previously shared their knowledge of the cause of their elder daughter's death. They had not wanted to upset their surviving daughter when she was just ready to start school. Mary's father said that relatives took her on holiday immediately after Margaret's death 'just to give us time to recover'. On their younger child's return they took her to school and 'we just never talked about Margaret much'.

The painful silence following these words appeared to give the mother courage to express her greatest fear: that Mary would die from a brain tumour now that she too was 'having headaches and was the same age'. While the father consoled his wife, Mary began to talk about her 'owned' conscious depression.

After entering her comprehensive school, she had become more and more anxious about menstruation and feared becoming adult; she was the only one in the class without a boyfriend. Unconsciously she thought that she would die before her next birthday because she felt that she had no right to live longer than her dead sister. This, in turn, led to depressive feelings about what would happen to her parents if she died.

Depression and its links to school learning

Negative experiences of attachment behaviour can lead either to children entering school in a depressed state of mind, because they feel they are stupid or 'bad', or are too afraid to relate to others, or hold a belief that something dreadful will happen to themselves or their family members. Some children become depressed during their time in school. The latter group can be linked to ongoing experiences of further inappropriate adult behaviour towards them, either by older peers or members of a school staff. This can be a painful reminder of, for example, previous abuse or rejection within the home environment. Bullying, or even teasing by peers, can cause distress, as indeed can undue sarcasm or shouting from school staff.

Numerous authors have examined childhood depression in school-age children (see, for example Butler (1980); Colbert *et al.* (1982), Paananen and Jansen (1986)). Some focus on the effect this state has on aspects of children's learning, such as concentration and memorizing, and Maclausen and Quin (1976) look specifically at rotational errors in children's writing. Spence *et al.* (1989) and Osmond (1993) comment on the association with poor social skills.

Colbert *et al.* (1982), in their examination of learning disabilities and schoolchild depression, conclude that 'The number of depressed children of school age is far greater than is generally believed.' In their sample of 111 children in regular (mainstream) schooling, 71% were underachieving. These authors concluded that depression results in underachievement for intellectually capable children. They felt that 'Under-achieving and a facade of good behaviour may indicate undetected depression', but also that 'Teachers may be misdiagnosing depressed children as having a specific learning problem.' The children's 'failure to achieve in school was often mistaken for laziness, belligerence or in some cases a learning disability.' Osmond (1993) states that, 'Several researchers and clinicians have found a significant number of children with diagnosed learning difficulties who have co-occurring or even a primary depressive disorder.'

Stevenson and Romney (1984) take the personalities of non-depressed and depressed children into account in their exploratory research. They suggest that 'The personality traits which characterize the depressed LD [learning disabled] child; in particular high anxiety and low ego strength, point to a neurotic disposition.' Low self-esteem and 'oversensitivity', they feel, leads to difficulties in adjusting to social systems and 'may interfere with learning in the classroom and accentuate his[/her] academic problem'. Cohen (1985) in his consideration of adolescents with mild to moderately severe learning disabilities states that 'Low-level, chronic depression seems to be a psychological response to the experience of being learning-disabled.' The expectation of the behaviour of others towards them was also noted.

Clearly depression is related to a child's experience with significant attachment figures in different environments, which impacts upon the learning process at home and in school. The reference to attachment figures within the context of school may seem inappropriate but we have in mind the concept of an educational attachment figure as described by Barrett and Trevitt (1991). They cite the work of two marital therapists to support their idea that workers, within their professional boundaries, do adopt such a role. Mattinson and Sinclair (1979) suggest 'We were in effect offering ourselves as attachment figures. We came to believe that such a role was a prerequisite for change.' When children enter school in a state of 'owned' depression, they may, from their own life experiences, 'tune into' messages of depression from teachers. If this becomes interactive depression, we wonder how much positive energy is available to either child or teacher for the completion of cognitive tasks. Our observations of children in the clinic or the class-room suggests that, in order to manage their feelings of despair, some adopt a bright facade in an attempt to cheer the adult; others are over-solicitous and helpful. Many become angry and rejecting; others sink into their own depression and cannot play or interact with peers or teachers.

We think that these children have not had enough opportunities to 'update' their 'internal working models' (Bowlby's concepts) in their interactions with primary caregivers who have continually failed to meet their needs (Bowlby, 1973, 1980). Their perception of such a person's behaviour towards them continues to be negative or punitive. If their perception of a teacher's behaviour, whether it is verbal or non-verbal, reminds them of the previous attachment, then dynamic, depressive feelings must surely override any feeling of hope. Their self-image is one of being blameworthy, worthless, and never able to do or learn enough to satisfy themselves or their teachers.

Children in school may behave in several ways and, as we have previously indicated, this may be particular to the child's personality and/or related to a child's life circumstances. It can be a transitory reaction linked to events that have taken place in the classroom, the school, or its immediate environs. Such behaviours can signify symptoms of child-hood depression of a more serious nature. Livingston (1985) considered childhood depression from a psychiatric point of view. He recognized that a major depressive disorder (MDD) is associated with difficulties in learning and cognition. He diagnosed MDD as a combina-tion of symptoms, such as being sad or unstable, exhibiting loss of inter-est or pleasure in usual activities (he says that this must persist for at least two weeks), with at least four of the general depressive behaviours listed below present over time. This opinion is also expressed by Goodyer (1993).

Overt behaviours

- Aggressive behaviour;
- robotic behaviour;
- lethargic behaviour;
- anger;
- tearful behaviour;
- bullying;

- adopting role of victim/'baby';
- hyperactivity/inability to stay with task;
- hiding;
- non-attendance;
- indifference to peer group;
- verbal abuse;
- denigration of others, including spitting;
- rushing around/out of control;
- physiological complaints.

Covert behaviours

- Secretiveness (for example, concealing work);
- 'sly' hurt of peers;
- minimal capacity for play/interaction;
- 'downbeat' stance and/or facial expression;
- lack of initiative/decision-taking;
- short attention span/no sustained interest in task;
- wetting/soiling;
- irritability;
- low self-worth;
- tiredness;
- poor punctuality/little temporal sense;
- loss of energy/apathy;
- 'laziness';
- psychosomatic illness;
- farting;
- humming.

Hidden factors

- Fear of death/enforced loss of attachment figure
- fear of own death (violation by other);
- loss of appetite;
- nightmares/broken sleep;
- nocturnal enuresis;
- suicidal behaviour;
- feelings of guilt;
- separation anxiety;
- unwilling to hear.

Verbal indicators

- 'F ... off' ('I'm rubbish'; this shows a need to confirm self-denigration in order to feel alive);

- 'She did it, I never' (a need to blame others because admitting a 'bad' self-image would be intolerable);
- 'Can't think' (the capacity to think is unbearable; this is linked to abuse or distorted loss);
- 'I don't know' ('I don't want to know; if I find out I may not be able to handle this information');
- 'Oh! why bother? What's the point?' ('I have no control over my life');
- 'I'll do it, it'll be great' ('notice me, I may not be bad').
- 'Yea, yea, yea' ('this is so boring I don't want to hear it', equated with 'I am depressed and cannot take it in');
- 'It's hopeless' ('I'm helpless');
- 'I'm fine' (denial).

The common factor in our listed behaviours (which cannot be regarded in any way as exhaustive) is that they represent, primarily, a child's internalized self image as 'bad' or worthless, as 'rubbish', or weak or out of control. The child's perception of self, and self with other, seems to have been set, and has not been modified or updated positively.

How can the adult manage childhood depression in school?

Certain behaviours from children or young people elicit certain behaviour within ourselves. If we find aggressiveness, tearfulness or indifference in the class difficult to tolerate we are likely to control a negative reaction by developing a defensive response. It is impossible, when working with a large group, to respond to children or young people in a way that they recognize as meeting their individual difficulties or hurt. Colbert *et al.* (1982) put forward several reasons for an adult's non-recognition of behaviours that can be associated with depression.

1: Children mask their distress in an effort to avoid upsetting adults.
2: Adults prefer to avoid dealing with the feelings of guilt aroused by depression in their children, whom they might have neglected or mistreated.
3: The child's unhappiness evokes a sadness in the adult, which may already be nearly overwhelming.
4: The depression of children is mixed with a persistent hope for relief, which manifests itself as a high level of attention-demanding activity.

We have chosen two more families to illustrate the concepts of anxious attachment; owned, received, or interactive depression which we feel contribute to inhibited functioning and learning.

Matthew

Matthew, aged nine, was referred to an educational therapist by his school at the instigation of his mother. The family consisted of a mother, a father, and a sister aged ten-and-a-half. Since the birth of her daughter, the mother had experienced long bouts of depression. Matthew was the result of an unplanned pregnancy. The family lived abroad until Matthew entered school, which meant that the mother lost her network of friends. She had no parents or extended family. Matthew's mother was able to meet his physical needs, but his father was more emotionally available to him and thus became his primary attachment figure. The family returned to England when Matthew began school; the father changed his occupation to one which kept him away from home for long periods.

Matthew in the classroom

His teacher described Matthew in school as 'being in a world of his own'. He showed no interest in school tasks, group activities, information gathering, sharing, or sustained concentration in work or play. In the playground his behaviour oscillated between being a bully or a victim; at other times he chose to isolate himself.

Matthew at home

During family meetings, which his father was unable to attend, his mother described his behaviour at home as 'causing mayhem'. He placed himself in danger by locking himself in the family car, by dismantling electrical appliances, or playing dangerously with ropes. These events were regularly regaled to father by telephone. The mother attempted to cope with this behaviour by trying to keep Matthew within her sight at all times. In our opinion she became a 'smothering' mother, but this behaviour alternated with leaving him for long periods with newly acquired 'friends'. Recounting of these events exercised the mother and daughter to the extent that family meetings were dominated by them and Matthew adopted the role of a clown. The mother's reaction to her son's behaviour led to a 'mismatch of their approaches to one another' (Barrett and Trevitt, 1991). The lack of synchronicity was demonstrated by Matthew's clowning when mother became despairing; when he showed that he was in touch with his depressed feelings mother jollied him back into the clowning role.

Matthew in the clinic

In his first sessions with his educational therapist he began in a state of spinning hyperactivity. This rapidly dissipated into a state of intense despair. He slumped in his chair, in contrast to his earlier animation, and showed no interest in learning. This behaviour was rapidly followed by tales of fantasy, feelings of sickness, or 'jokey' comments. The educational therapist recognized this as a manifestation of depression, but did not collude with Matthew's defensive clowning behaviour or his attempts to deflect from the task, but stayed with Matthew's feelings of hopelessness. She felt that Matthew was expressing his depression in 'an obscured or masked form' ... 'through the substitution of one activity normally associated with depression by one not so obviously connected' (Higgins, 1992). After several months, Matthew gradually began to interact and showed brief enjoyment in a shared task. During one of his sessions he chose to draw a house with no doors or other means of entry. It was empty except for one lone figure in an upstairs window. This drawing was captioned 'the house and the boy are sad, there is no-one around'. Once Matthew was able to share and acknowledge his depression he showed a marginal interest in reading. He began by cutting out cards and writing the words he wished to learn on them. He placed corresponding illustrations beneath each. However, when he chose the word 'mum' he inverted the middle letter and drew the illustration on the back. (No other words had inverted letters.) Once this task was completed, Matthew asked for the cards to be looked after by the educational therapist. Over a period of several weeks, he took them out of his box to look at them, and very slowly began to make the perceptual leap towards reading them. This progress could not be sustained when his mother experienced a depressive episode, particularly if this coincided with his father being away from home.

Robert

Robert, aged 14, suffered a growth hormone deficiency which resulted in a small, immature stature. He was referred to an adolescent unit by his parents at the request of the school. The presenting problems were Robert's attacking and provoking behaviour, his failure to learn, and his refusal to record work in the classroom or to accept that he had homework. The parents saw the meetings that were offered as a means of 'sorting out' their son's educational problem and as a forum to discuss moving him to another school (there had been two recent changes for similar educational and social problems).

He presented in a pseudo-adult role, saying he attended any activities on his own, did not come home on time, and did not go where he had told his parents he would be. His conversation was interspersed with adult platitudes ('oh well, that's life') and he was overinvolved in the discussion of adult business, which was in direct contrast to his small stature and his child-like anticipation and excitement about the forthcoming sessions. We were to see this dichotomous behaviour throughout the family meetings. Robert's immediate family consisted of the mother and her second husband, who was considerably younger and for whom this was a first marriage. The mother was a cleaner and father worked away from home for several nights a week. There was no evidence of any extended family or network of friends.

The first family meeting

Robert's father was angry and highly critical of his son's behaviour, blaming him for causing problems and not being grateful for parental efforts. His behaviour toward the unit team, an educational and an art therapist, was hostile. He complained about the effect on his wife of Robert's behaviour, as if he was powerless to intervene and devoid of adult or parental authority. The mother was unable to stop the paternal tirade, and denied that Robert was 'so bad'. She appeared emotionally dead and detached, although was obviously the physical 'carer' for Robert, who was well groomed. Robert became animated whenever his father spoke, seeming to prefer criticism to a lack of attention, but he rarely looked at his mother. It was interesting to note that Robert was reported as refusing to eat food cooked by his mother, preferring to make himself toast, but when the father was at home, the father cooked the meals, which the family enjoyed eating together, although Robert was 'always late to the table'.

The assessment

The educational therapist assessed Robert's learning profile in order to explore any indicators of his resistance to learning and teaching and to reassure the family that the educational problems were being taken seriously. In the two one-to-one sessions, Robert was interested, keen and co-operative, and not afraid to say what he found hard although there was some fantasy about his successes. His profile showed peaks and troughs in performance levels and indicated immaturity in contrast to his chronological age. (This immaturity was belied by his grasp of concepts in other sessions that were not educationally focused.) The school suspected that he might be dyslexic but the assessment did not indicate a specific learning difficulties pattern. His Goodenough 'Draw a Man Test' (1926) showed an immature figure with no ears and rigid arms which seemed unable to move. Although it is inadvisable to make judgements about children's drawings in a categoric way, this portrayal confirmed the team's feeling that Robert's capacity for learning had become frozen. Emotional factors were inhibiting Robert's developmental progress and the functioning of the family system. Questions were raised as to what it was that the family found difficult to hear, or what did not make sense to them when heard.

With some reluctance the parents agreed to Robert having four individual sessions with the art therapist whilst the family sessions were continued. Robert was excited about the prospect of the individual sessions and arrived early for every one. In the first he painted a very controlled picture of an isolated church on an island surrounded by rough water. Both therapists were forcibly struck by the loneliness and desolation in this painting. He wanted to show it to his parents but decided they wouldn't like it. When he told them about it his father responded by saying 'That's not going to help you to do your school work.' His mother made no response.

In the second session there were indicators of depressive feelings. He spoke of how close he felt to his brother who had not visited the family home for three years. In the next family session the therapists mentioned the surprise they had felt on learning that Robert had a brother (Robert had given permission for this to be shared). Both parents made little of this fact, and said he was an older half-brother from mother's previous marriage who visited them briefly but with whom they were now out of contact. The mother became more subdued at this point, but father said it was 'just one of those family things'. Did Robert and his mother retain some hope of a relationship which they had subsequently lost? Had Robert not understood the departure and had he therefore idealized the brief relationship?

It was later revealed that the mother also had a daughter from her previous marriage, whom Robert did not know, although he knew of her existence. Both of these children had remained with their father at the break-up of the mother's first marriage and were now adults in their twenties. The daughter's own marriage had also broken down and the child of that marriage had remained with its father. The therapists expressed their sense of Robert's sadness and isolation, and mentioned the feelings of loss and unresolved grief that might be preventing him from learning. His father made a link at this juncture, recognizing that Robert could learn with him but that Robert could not remember things when he had to undertake them by himself. 'It seems as if he cannot cope on his own.'

This marked the turn in Robert's relationship with his father, who explored, with his son, ways in which his social and educational life could be changed. The father took control and became a guiding parental figure. Robert joined the Army Cadets, which he enjoyed immensely and where he learned enough to pass examinations. Father also expressed his belief that Robert should stay at the same school and try to change the pattern of his experiences. They worked out a system of monitoring homework and allowing free time and the father changed his position at work to allow him more time at home.

Throughout this period of transition and change, Robert's pictures changed to ones of holidays and fantasy fun, followed by space aliens and expressions of conflict and anger. Later work showed a messy regression in flowing, dripping, thick paint – these pictures had an animation and life about them which Robert recognized and enjoyed.

He painted a flag which represented his emerging sense of identity and self-worth. Robert altered his behaviour patterns of non-attentiveness and lack of interest; he regained his lost capacity for thinking and reduced his declarations of boredom mixed with hyperactivity, lethargy, withdrawal, low self-worth and denigration of peers. He began to learn 'within the relationship' and behave in a manner more appropriate to his age through the father's capacity to 'hold him in mind' (Winnicott, 1965), but his anxious attachment to his mother remained. At school he found a small nucleus of friends with whom he identified and met regularly on Saturdays.

Robert's non-learning state and his social problems seemed to be manifestations of his owned and received depression and his anxious attachment to his parents. His mother was present but emotionally unavailable, her depression partially linked to her first 'lost' family; his father kept disappearing and reappearing but the interactive depression was exacerbated by the uncertainties of the marital relationship, the parenting roles, both past and present, and the tenuous state of the family attachment system.

Concluding comments

During the preparation of this chapter we were concerned that many authors and researchers have already used a number of the criteria that we had considered as constituting significant features of depression, based on our own work. We note, however, that there is a school of thought that educators can be trained to recognize depression in children and young people, at any point on our continuum. Goodyer (1993) examined pupil depression in schools and stated that the condition occurs '... more often than most schools realise'. Following a brief review of what was known about depression in the school population, he added, most importantly in our opinion, 'that teachers may have an important role in detecting serious depression in young people and contributing to their assessment and management.' He emphasized that teachers, rather than parents, may well be the first to observe features related to depressive illness. Children and young people may 'show alterations in mood and behaviour with peers in school, as well as lowered performance in class', although he comments on the difficulty of differentiating a 'transient upset in everyday life' from a serious clinical condition. He also advocates offering postgraduate training to those teachers who have an interest in a therapeutic approach to their work. As educational therapy training tutors, we agree, and especially with his emphasis on the need for such work to be supervised in order to avoid overidentification with a child's or young person's 'problem'. 'If this happens counsellors may lose their objectivity and say and do things that may not be in the child's interest' (Goodyer, 1993).

We had not fully appreciated, when we began writing, the importance of helping children to know

> that they are depressed and [will] respond to an educational approach in which an expert gives them a description of depression, including what we understand about its nature and effects and which aspects of this information are relevant to them. Children appreciate being told they are suffering from an illness which is not their fault.' (Goodyer, 1993)

Our previous work as members of multidisciplinary teams leads us to agree with Goodyer's suggestion that schools taking a therapeutic approach should develop a working relationship with those working in child and adolescent mental health.

We referred at the beginning of the chapter to articles addressed to the general public, alerting parents to signs of depression in their children and young people. There is a wealth of research on this painful subject and its effect on early learning and increasing concern is now being expressed that it often remains a hidden factor affecting later learning in schools and colleges. If we add this knowledge to our own experience of working with members of mental health teams, there would seem to be a powerful argument for alerting all personnel in the field of education to the long-term dangers of the frequently unidentified state of mind, depression.

References

Barrett M, Trevitt J (1991) Attachment Behaviour and the Schoolchild – An Introduction to Educational Therapy. London: Routledge.

Bowlby J (1969) 'Attachment'. In Attachment and Loss 1. London: Hogarth Press and Institute of Psychoanalysis; New York: Basic Books.

Bowlby J (1973) Separation: anxiety and anger. In Attachment and Loss 2. London: Hogarth Press and Institute of Psychoanalysis; New York: Basic Books.

Bowlby J (1979) On knowing what you are supposed to know and feeling what you are not supposed to feel. Canadian Journal of Psychiatry 24: 403–8.

Bowlby J (1980) Loss: sadness and depression. In Attachment and Loss 3. London: Hogarth Press and Institute of Psychoanalysis; New York: Basic Books.

Bowlby J (1982) Attachment and loss: retrospect and prospect. American Journal of Orthopsychiatry 52: 664–78.

Bowlby J (1988) Secure Base. London: Routledge & Kegan Paul.

Butler LF (1980) Depressive child in the classroom. Orbit: Ideas About Teaching and Learning 11(2): 24–5.

Cohen J (1985) Learning Disabilities and adolescence: developmental considerations. Adolescent Psychiatry 12: 177–96.

Cohen NJ (1991) Recognised and unrecognised language impairment in psychologically disturbed children: child symptomology, maternal depression and family dysfunction. Canadian Journal of Behavioural Science 23(3) pp. 376–88.

Colbert P, Newman B, Ney P, and Young J (1982) Learning disabilities as a symptom of depression in children. Journal of Learning Disabilities 15: 333–6.

Coleman JC (1980) The Nature of Adolescence. London: Methuen.

Dalley MB, Bolocofsky DN, Alcorn MB, Baker C (1992) Depressive syptomatology, attributable style, dysfunctional attitude, and social competency in adolescents with and without learning disabilities. School Psychology Review 3: 444–58.

Deri SK (1984) Symbolization and Creativity. Madison CT: International Universities Press.

Ferriman A (1995) Telegraph Magazine, 7 October, London.

Freud S (1955) Mourning and Melancholia. Standard Edition 14. London: Hogarth Press.

Goodenough FL (1926) Measurement of Intelligence by Drawings. New York: Harcourt Brace and World.

Goodyer IM (1990) Family relationships, life events and childhood psychopathology. Journal of Child Psychiatry 31(1): 161–87.

Goodyer IM (1993) Depression among pupils at school. British Journal of Special Education 20(2): 51–4.

Higgins R. (1992) The secret life of the depressed child. In Varma V (Ed) The Secret Life of Vulnerable Children. London: Routledge.

Hooper SR, Hynd GW, Mattison RE (Eds) (1992) Child Psychopathology: Diagnostic Criteria and Clinical Assessment. Hillsdale NJ: Lawrence Erlbaum Associates.

Johnson K (1989) Trauma in the Lives of Children. London: Macmillan.

Kyle R (1995) The Independent, 23 August, London.

Law L. (1996) Bringing educational therapy into the classroom. In Barrett M, and Varma V (Eds) Every Picture Tells a Story. London: Whurr Publishers.

Livingston R (1985) Depressive illness and learning difficulties: research needs and practical implications. In Journal of Learning Disabilities 18(9): 518–21.

Maag JW, Behrens JT, DiGangi SA (1992) Dysfunctional cognitions associated with adolescent depression: Findings across special populations. Exceptionality 3(1): 31–47.

Maag JW and Reid R (1994) The phenomenology of depression among students with and without learning disabilities: more similar than different. In Learning Disabilities Research and Practice 9(2) 91–103.

Macauslan A, Quin V (1976) The rotation of confusable letters in the writing of depressed children. Child-care Health Development 2 (November/December): 379–86.

Mind Publications (1994) Understanding Childhood Distress. London.

Mind Publications (1994) Understanding Depressions. London.

Mind Publication (1994) Understanding Post-Natal Depression. London.

Mind Publication (1994) Understanding Manic Depression. London.

Morgan SR (1994) At Risk Youth in Crises: a Team Approach in the Schools (second edition). Austin TX: Pro-Ed.

Morris ML (1980–81) Childhood depression in the primary grades: early identification, a teacher consultation remedial model and classroom correlates of change. Interchange 11(1): 61–75.

Murray L (1988) Effects of post-natal depression on infant development: direct studies of early mother/infant interaction. In Kumar R, Brockington IF (Eds) Mothers and Mental Illness 2; Causes and Consequences. London: Wright.

Murray L, Trevarthen I (1986) The infant's role in mother/infant communication. Journal of Children's Language 13: 15–29.

Osman B (1993) Learning disabilities and depression in childhood. In Field K, Kaufman E, Saltzman B (Eds) Emotions and Learning Reconsidered. New York: Gardner Press.

Paananen N, Janzen HL (1986) Incidence and characteristics of depression in elementary school children. Canadian Journal of School Psychology 2(1): 7–9.

Prima (1994) February. London.

Rie HE (1966) Depression in childhood: a survey of some pertinent contributions. Journal of the American Academy of Child Psychiatry 5: 553–83.

Salzberger-Wittenberg I (1991) Psycho-analytic Insight and Relationships. London: Routledge.

Semrud-Clikeman M, Hynd GW (1991) Review of issues and measures in childhood depression. School Psychology International 12(4): 275–98.

Shulman S, Fisch RO, Zempel CE, Gadish O (1991) Children with phenylketonuria: the interface of family and child functioning. Journal of Developmental and Behavioural Pediatrics 12(5): 315–21.

Snyder J, Huntley D. (1990) Troubled families and troubled youth: the development of antisocial behaviour and depression in children. In Leone PE (Ed) Understanding Troubled and Troubling Youth. Newbury Park CA: Sage Publications.

Spence SH, Hensley R, Kennedy E (1989) An examination of the relationship between childhood depression and social competence amongst primary school children. Journal of Child Psychology and Psychiatry 30(4): 561–73.

Stevenson OT, Romney DM (1984) Depression in learning disabled children. Journal of Learning Disabilities 17: 579–82.

Waterfield J, Brown A (1996) Educational therapy in the clinic and the classroom. In Barrett M, Varma V (Eds) Every Picture Tells a Story. London: Whurr Publishers.

Winnicott DW (1965) The Maturational Process and the Facilitating Environment. London: Hogarth Press.

Wolkind S (1984) A longitudinal study of maternal depression and childhood behaviour problems. In Journal of Child Psychology and Psychiatry 25(1): 91–109.

Young Mind Information Service (1994) Children and Young People Get Depressed Too ... . London: Young Minds Trust.

Chapter 8
Depression in Childhood and Adolescence in Primary Health Care

GRAHAM CURTIS JENKINS

Working as a general practitioner pediatrician, the author developed a comprehensive child care service, over a thirty-year period, for children under five years old in the 18,000 patient practice in which he worked (Curtis Jenkins, 1976; Curtis Jenkins, Andren and Collins, 1978). He was privileged to be able to observe the varieties of normal development and growth in children at first hand over extended periods in the practice's child and family consultation service and to develop an understanding of how to help young children and their parents who consulted him for a variety of problems (Curtis Jenkins, 1982).

The primary care pediatric team consisted of a midwife, four health visitors, the author, and a part-time community pediatrician. Families with problems could make an appointment at the child and family consultation service to see the health visitor in the first instance. After this initial meeting they were invited to make an appointment for a consultation with the author. Both parents were encouraged to attend and about 20% of consultations took place with both parents present. An enormous variety of problems and disorders were brought by parents.

As part of the service developed in the practice, the author carried out a routine initial home visit to every newborn baby and was able to help parents interpret and understand what they had already noticed about their new child. When the author began the service in the mid-1960s, newborn babies were 'not allowed' to see or hear and all smiles were said to be caused 'by wind'. However, even at that time, some parents knew better and, despite the scorn of their family and friends, they persisted in believing that newborn babies could really copy their facial expressions, avert their gaze from a silent observing face, smile, and turn across a room to listen selectively to their mother's voice in preference to another. The author was usually able to confirm that their observations were correct (Curtis Jenkins and Newton, 1981). As the author became privy to problems and behavioural variants that never

124

featured in the textbooks of the time, the child and family consultation service came to be seen as a valuable resource by the families registered with the practice. To find out which interventions worked and which did not, and to discover how to support the parents in their often difficult and sometimes not so rewarding task of nurturing the growth and development of their children was difficult at first, with few guidelines or helpful hints in the textbooks of the time. However, with the help of parents and colleagues, the team developed a range of skills and strategies that helped both children and parents and which were acceptable to the parents (Curtis Jenkins, 1992).

As the team became more skilled in helping parents manage and cope with infants and young children with a range of often acute and suddenly developing behavioural disturbances of all kinds, it learned the importance of taking a careful history and focusing on the environment and the circumstances surrounding the genesis of such disturbances in order to develop helping strategies. The following case histories demonstrate the variety of presentations of depressive illness seen by the author in general practice and the need for all members of the primary care team who work with children and families to be aware of the ways in which depression, for instance, presents, and the ways in which children and families can be helped.

Case history 1

Sharon P arrived with both parents at the child and family consultation clinic. Sharon was the first-born child, now 9 months old, of Mr P a tool setter and Mrs P who had worked at a local engineering company as personal assistant to the managing director until Sharon was born. (The family were well known to the author because he cared for Mrs P's mother who lived next door to her daughter.) On arrival, Sharon first hid her head in her mother's shoulder and then watched me suspiciously out of her tear-stained eyes. She looked frightened and her movements were listless. The overwhelming impression was one of misery. The parents revealed that 6 weeks before Sharon had gone on holiday with them to Spain. As they boarded the plane Sharon became at first apprehensive and then cried inconsolably until the plane landed. She clung to her mother continuously and wouldn't allow her father to hold her on the bus to the resort hotel. On the first evening the parents decided to go out for a meal and used the hotel's babysitter service. They expected no problems as Sharon had always fallen asleep quickly at home. When the Spanish-speaking babysitter arrived Sharon was still wide awake and tearful and wouldn't let her mother go. She was finally transferred screaming to the babysitter's waiting arms by her father. On their return home some hours later Sharon's screams could be heard in the hotel foyer and when her parents got her to their bedroom Sharon was crying uncontrollably. The babysitter was very upset because she was sure that the parents would assume she had not done her job properly. Mrs P picked Sharon up and, after a long time crying, the baby fell asleep in her mother's arms. She awoke three hours later. From that moment she never let her mother out of her sight. Any attempt by her mother at leaving her, even to go to the toilet, was met with tears and distress. She refused to sleep in her own bed and Mr P described the holiday as a 'real nightmare'.

Worse was to follow. On return from Spain, Mrs P's mother called round and, when confronted by a clinging, distressed child who wouldn't look at her and who refused to allow her to pick her up, she said crossly, 'You've been spoiling her. What she wants is to be left to cry it out.' The advice seemed to make things worse and Sharon became more and more distressed as the days went by. She continued to sleep fitfully, only falling asleep in her mother's arms and waking immediately if her mother attempted to put her down. She had 'gone off' her food and had stopped smiling and laughing. Mr P remarked that she had stopped 'talking back' to them. Mrs P finished the story by remarking 'It's as if she's terribly sad doctor', quickly following up what she perceived to be a stupid remark with the words 'but of course little babies can't get sad, can they doctor?'

I was able to explain to the parents that Sharon was feeling very keenly acute separation and stranger anxiousness and that some experts thought that children this young could become depressed (Bowlby, 1988). Her watchful, terrified and grief-stricken demeanour was the outward manifestation of her emotional state. Her behaviour, trusting no one, not allowing her mother or (to a lesser extent) her father out of her sight for even a moment was the only way she knew of controlling the situation and was an extreme example of normal behaviour seen in many children at this age. The parents gratefully received the interpretation I gave them about what was going on as 'it explained it all' in Mrs P's words.

The interventions I made were simple and direct. Over the next few weeks Sharon slowly became her old self, smiling and cheerful and trusting me enough finally to play with me on her clinic visits. We encouraged some gradual attitudinal changes in the rest of the family, supported by the health visitor who saw the other family members to explain what was happening and to help them support Mr and Mrs P. A diary kept by Mrs P enabled her and the team to watch the progress made. The family interventions were an essential part of the treatment (Bowlby, 1988; Estrada and Pinsof, 1995; Mutale, 1994).

Sharon occasionally had further brief episodes of misery and sadness over the next 15 years, until the family moved away from the area. Mrs P was usually able to identify the causes and help Sharon resolve the problems as and when they recurred. The recurring theme was that sudden change of all kinds caused Sharon to feel insecure and this triggered her depressed reaction.

Case history 2

With the development of the under-five service the author became drawn into the diagnosis and management of problems and disorders developing in older children.

Jonathan S was a third child whom the author had delivered at home to Mrs S. She was a cheerful East Ender who had come to live in the local community with her parents and six brothers and sisters when they were bombed during the Second World War. Mrs S was a cleaner, and her husband worked as a dustman. Jonathan, at his four-and-a-half-year-old pre-school check had appeared confident and loquacious. Signs of his delayed acquisition of cerebral dominance and his slight difficulties with the standard test of auditory sequential memory which was used in the developmental surveillance programme were noted at the time. They hinted that he might have some difficulties in acquiring reading and writing skills at school and it was suggested to the mother that if he did have problems he could return to the learning difficulties clinic run in the practice after one year in school to see how he was doing.

Jonathan was never ill and the author was pleasantly surprised to meet a well built, tall nine year old one day during a routine general practice consulting session four years later. It was apparent that something was very wrong, however. He sat slumped listlessly on his chair, tearful and miserable. His mother reported that, for about four months, Jonathan had been refusing to go to school. He cried frequently and was often found by his mother crying alone in his room. He had lost his appetite and she thought he had lost weight. He frequently wandered around the home at night saying that he couldn't sleep. The previous night Jonathan had told his mother that he wanted to die. To the question 'It must be very difficult for you feeling so sad all the time. When do you feel at your worst?' Jonathan hesitated for a moment as he reflected on the question and then replied 'I'm worst when I first wake up but it gets no better all day' and he began to cry silently, tears falling down his cheeks unchecked. To the author's questions about his reading and writing progress at school he replied 'it's alright'. A quick test of his reading and spelling skills, however, showed that he only recognized a few of his letters and couldn't write his name. His inability had been noticed not only by his form teacher but by all the other children in the class who had nicknamed him 'Dumb Dumb'. His life at school was, in his words 'horrible'. His mother was appalled when she heard Jonathan describe the situation at school. 'I'm going down there to sort them out' was her immediate reaction. The author explained to Jonathan that he wasn't stupid but that reading and spelling was very difficult for some people if their brain couldn't work in the required way. Later, at the author's learning difficulties clinic (Curtis Jenkins, 1979), when a full assessment was carried out, Jonathan brightened slightly as he and his mother began to understand what his problems might be. An in-depth educational psychological assessment was arranged and the school was alerted to the bullying. Jonathan remained profoundly depressed, however. His appetite remained poor, he frequently cried and talked about death and dying. He was seen with his mother frequently every 4–5 days. No medication was given. It proved impossible to obtain an appointment with a child psychiatrist for 14 weeks. Seven weeks after the first consultation and nearly six months from the onset of his depressive episode he suddenly and dramatically improved and decided for himself that he did not need to return to see the author again but thought he would keep his appointment 'to get my spelling sorted out' with the educational psychologist.

A possible explanation for the sudden recovery revealed itself when the author remembered that Jonathan's father had been seen three years earlier with a severe depressive illness lasting eight months which had been relieved by appropriate antidepressant medication. The family moved to another town soon after so the author was not able to observe whether Jonathan's illness was the first episode of lifelong recurring depressive illness.

Case history 3

The following case history is important because it describes the way in which depressive illness is so often missed in older children.

One November evening, Tom E and his wife arrived to consult the author. 'She says I need to have my head examined', he remarked bitterly as his wife began to explain the reason for coming. Tom E was a 29-year-old self-employed builder who worked very hard to keep his family, wife and two children in some style. The house resembled a building site for most of the time as ever more ambitious extensions were added to their small detached cottage. He had only occasionally consulted over the years for minor ailments. Tom and his wife recounted the story of his recent change in behaviour. He had been unable to sleep for about 4 months, waking very early in the morning with his mind full of black depressing thoughts about his job and his family. He remarked: 'I can't seem to get my brain in gear until the middle of the afternoon.' Consequently he started late in the mornings and was falling behind on his current building contract. He described his lack of interest in sex and his concerns about death and dying, saying 'I know it's stupid doctor but I just can't stop thinking about blackness all the time.' He had thought about killing himself but couldn't for the sake of his wife and children.

The diagnosis of depression was obvious and antidepressant medication was chosen that enabled him to work without danger to himself and others around him. 'I've had feelings like this before doctor', Tom added, and as I began to write out a prescription he went on to describe four episodes throughout his teenage years and early twenties when he felt deeply depressed and had entertained thoughts of killing himself. He described seeing a variety of doctors for his physical complaints of loss of energy, tiredness and sleeplessness, but he did not trust them enough to tell them of his wanting to die 'because I knew they would tell me to pull myself together and I knew that wouldn't work as I had tried it already.' Tom E's illness lasted eight months before a spontaneous recovery occurred and he left off his antidepressant medication.

On perusal of his notes it was salutary to note that I was one of the doctors he had consulted in his teens and I had failed to detect the real reasons for consultation.

These three patients demonstrate the variety of presentations of depressive episodes in children and adolescents in general practice. They also point to the many factors which can trigger episodes. The histories of adults who suffer from depressive episodes suggest that at least some patients have a lifelong tendency to suffer depressive episodes, with or without so-called triggers. Stories like these are heard quite frequently in general practice.

During the author's medical training nobody had mentioned the possibility that children became depressed, so he was initially unable to frame these children's distress in such terms. Yet, by attempting to understand the developmental situations present in both these children's lives, and by a process of self-education and learning, it became possible, with the support of able health visitor colleagues, first to recognize the condition and then to engineer changes and facilitate solutions.

In the case of Jonathan P, the antecedent trigger was provisionally identified and the problem apparently resolved, but the depressive episode ran its course. Tom E could not trust anyone during his teenage years with what he thought was his guilty secret and his somatizing presentation was not recognized. Unfortunately, Tom E's story is a common one and experience shows the difficulty all health services have in reaching out to teenagers.

Between 70% and 80% of teenagers think of themselves as completely healthy, and evidence from North America and Britain reveals that there is a mutual lack of communication between teenagers and general practitioners (Curtis Jenkins, 1979). Teenagers often do not trust general practitioners because they think they will pass on information about them to their parents. General practitioners feel helpless when yet another inarticulate teenager gives monosyllabic answers to their questions.

So how can a general practitioner work to improve trust, demon-strate concern, and address the problems of childhood and adolescent depressive illness?

The HEADSS system, developed in California, has been shown to cover the key concerns felt by teenagers. The questions are carefully framed to move from the personal to the intimate and general practi-tioners and others have found the technique valuable in trying to find out what is going on in teenagers' minds (Smith, 1992).

H – home – 'Are you able to talk to your parents?'
E – education – Ask for actual grades and marks.
A – activities – Ask about friends and friendship.
D – drugs – Explain why you are asking.
S – sex – Explain why you are asking.
S – suicide – Ask only if answers to the previous questions suggest a risk.

Finding out is vital if we are to help. Despite the fact that it is well known that children and adolescents suffer from a range of common, persistent and handicapping mental disorders (Williams, 1993; Jacobson, Wilkinson and Owen, 1994; Epstein, Rice and Wallace, 1989; Bowman and Garralda, 1993) and general practitioners see children frequently for a variety of health-related reasons, rarely, on current evidence, do they look for or detect distress and mental disorders.

Some experiments point the way forward. Frequent attenders commonly have comorbidity and a variety of strategies have now been developed to address the problem of underdetection of mental disor-der. Coverley *et al.* (1995) used a structured single session intervention for use in general practice settings with mothers of children with newly diagnosed mental health problems. The intervention targeted mothers of frequent attenders who had been identified in a previous study. It aimed to boost parental confidence and to help parents develop a management style for dealing with the reported difficulties. Two thirds of the mothers who stayed the course found intervention useful or very useful at follow-up. The children's behaviour showed no change but there was a weak correlation with reduced general practitioner consul-tations in families who said that they had benefited.

Westman, in an unpublished study (Westman, 1995), reported a different strategy. The clinic in the study aimed to identify adolescents with a high risk of depressive disorder and to offer a psychotherapeutic intervention. Out of the 100 young people invited by letter an astonish-ing 25% attended, but for the most part they only attended because their parents were not invited too. Eleven of the attenders had a depressive disorder and Westman estimated that the majority of children diagnosed as suffering form a mental disorder would have a depressive type illness.

Four of the 11 received the intervention and three reported subjective improvement. What was important was that 10 of the 11 attenders had visited the practice in the previous year for health problems but their mental health problems had remained undetected.

What, then, is the true incidence of depressive disorders in children and adolescents? Until recently it was thought that depression was rare in childhood and that it increased in frequency after the onset of puberty. It is now known that the incidence of depression in boys appears constant across the child and adolescent age span but increases for girls (Cooper and Goodyer, 1993) with a reported prevalence of 1.9% in primary school children, rising to 4.7% in adolescents (Todd and Geller, 1995). It is probable that, when an adolescent develops a depressive episode and becomes 'clinically depressed', he can expect further episodes by the time he reaches the age of 21 years. If the adolescent has an immediate relative suffering from clinical depression then he or she has a two or three times greater chance of suffering from depression.

Adolescent depressive episodes are often linked to recent life events, as in the case histories described (Dadds, Schwatz and Sauders, 1987). Events that entail loss or a profound threat to self-esteem are particularly common triggers, but as the second case history demonstrated, the episodes are not necessarily caused by them. Poor social support and the absence of a network of peers and friends further increase vulnerability. Many male teenagers with recurring episodes do not present so clearly. For instance, criminality can be an outward manifestation of a masked depressive illness. Aggression and moodiness, often noted by immediate family members, are pointers, as is hypersomnia. What follows, particularly in environments lacking strong family structures and secure social support, is a descent into recurring criminality and substance misuse as the adolescent acts out hopelessness and low self-esteem. It should come as no surprise to observe the high death rates for suicide in young offenders' establishments in Britain. These suggest that depressed young persons have found the only solution to their sense of hopelessness and worthlessness in what they see as an uncaring society.

Tylee (1994) estimates that no more than 2% of children with depressive episodes are recognized, despite the fact that they often present to general practitioners with physical problems which are taken at face value or dismissed as 'teenager problems'. So what can the individual general practitioner and the rest of the primary care team do to correct this unsatisfactory state of affairs?

First, it is vital to take a good history with infants and young children and to ascertain what the parents noticed at the time the child's behaviour changed (as in the first case history). Secondly, it is important to remember that, in older children, the most common signs are social withdrawal and lack of involvement in normal activities – stopping homework, school refusal and giving up sporting activities. Changes in sleep are not constant: hypersomnia as well as the classic early morning insomnia can occur with equal frequency. Changes in eating habits, either eating little or too much, are sometimes present and it is important to enquire specifically about energy levels as the fashionable diagnosis of chronic fatigue syndrome (ME) has often already been suggested by family and friends as an explanation for the symptoms. Expressions of worthlessness and even that 'life isn't worth living' are only heard if the general practitioner listens carefully enough and sensitively facilitates a discussion about feelings – always an embarrassing subject for teenagers at the best of times.

Practice guidelines for the management of childhood depression are still not standardized and probably never will be as each child needs to be viewed individually and developmentally (Kratochwill and Morris, 1993; Kazdin, 1995). It is probable that antidepressant medication is ineffective in all but the most seriously affected child and probably has no place at all in treating children before puberty (Hazell *et al.*, 1995). At puberty it is even more important to assess carefully the severity of depression. Misdiagnosis can have many consequences. The result of failure can be to leave a deeply distressed, isolated teenager in an alien, non-understanding environment of a family that itself feels rejected by the teenager's behaviour. This, in turn, can lead to criminal and destructive behaviour and even suicide.

Crisis intervention, solution-focused ways of working and cognitive approaches (Kendall, 1994) are all probably helpful methods of working with moderately depressed adolescents but they demand expert skill if they are to be applied with consistency and with the sensitivity required when working with teenagers. It is important to try to tease out antecedents that might have triggered the depressive episode and then work with the patient and parents to find solutions. The general practitioner can develop some of these skills and a few counsellors now entering general practice are appropriately trained to practise the techniques of cognitive-behavioural therapy (Dadds, Schwatz and Sauders, 1987), crisis intervention and solution-focused ways of working that are possibly of some effect. Training in systemic ways of working with children and their families is probably more useful (Estrada and Pinsof, 1995). A number of studies have demonstrated interpersonal psychotherapeutic approaches to be as effective as cognitive-behavioural therapeutic techniques in adults, but very few counsellors and other mental health professionals, psychologists or community psychiatric nurses have learned how to apply these styles of working and there is as yet little evidence that they are successful with children before puberty.

General practitioners usually start adolescents on antidepressant medication without prior referral when they have made a diagnosis of depression, contrary to the recommendation of some experts who believe that only specialists can make a diagnosis and manage medication. The older tricyclic antidepressants were and are unpleasant to take and adolescents find the side-effects unacceptable. This causes poor compliance. The newer serotonin reuptake inhibitors with their lower incidence of side-effects may cause adolescents fewer problems. It is important, however, to start with a low dose and slowly increase the dose over 2–3 weeks. This ensures compliance and enables the general practitioner to observe closely clinical signs of response and to stop the medication if it appears to be having no effect, continuing to watch carefully for any rebound of symptoms when medication has been stopped. The use of these drugs is still controversial and there are few well-performed studies to guide practice.

What future developments are needed before children and adolescents are appropriately diagnosed and treated? Reductions in national child surveillance programmes for children aged under five have, at a stroke, reduced the chances of detection of depressive episodes in this age group by reducing contacts with general practitioners and health visitors. Parents tend to see the lack of importance given to the developmental process of their children and the lack of interest by the professionals in the vagaries and variety of childhood behavioural disorders as evidence that it is not the primary care team's job to be interested. General practitioners, losing this chance of contact with children, can become deskilled. Health visitors, diminishing in numbers every year, and with ever fuller work schedules, have an impossible task to perform in educating and supporting parents and helping them when they and their children run into problems (HMSO, 1993). Few general practitioners have specific knowledge and understanding about what child psychotherapy can do. This makes it difficult for them to be clear about who, when, and why to refer children to specialist services where they exist. With long waiting lists and sometimes apparently ineffective ways of working, such referral seems a waste of time and money anyway to some general practitioners – an increasingly important fact to be taken into account with the advent of fundholding in British general practice and as purchasers are encouraged to make purchasing decisions based on evidence of benefit (Williams, 1992). Child and adolescent psychiatric services are set to grow in the United Kingdom, but it is essential that mutual understanding and collaborative ways of working are developed in the new managed care environment.

For instance, general practitioners report on the usefulness of a telephone consultation service that enables them to discuss difficult problems presenting in children. Specialists need to learn how to maximize the effects of interprofessional consultation, currently often bedevilled by turf wars between providers and purchasers. Recognition is an important intervention itself and can result in containment, explanation, and mobilization of family resources and, as Bowman and Garralda (1993) have pointed out, can reduce the likelihood of somatization.

General practitioners and child psychiatrists already agree that a family systems approach is the most appropriate way of working with depressed children and their families (Mutale, 1994) yet the number of family therapists shows no sign of increasing and only a tiny number of general practices employ a family therapist or run family therapy clinics in their practices.

The driving theme of educating the general practitioner and the primary care team must be that depression is common in childhood and adolescents, that it can occasionally be chronic, and that it can have unpredictable but usually harmful effects on the sufferers and their families if misdiagnosed. It also has considerable implications for the community. A variety of clinical interventions of proven efficacy, based on a sound knowledge of child development and its varieties and disorders, need to be developed and tested. The members of the primary care team also need to learn how to win the confidence of adolescents if they wish them to consult about feelings that the adolescents find difficult to understand and about which they are often ashamed. We need sound clinical trials of drug therapies before inflicting drugs of doubtful value on young people. There also needs to be a public awareness campaign not just run by health departments publishing leaflets but reaching out in other ways. The popular press, television – including soaps – are already being used to educate the public and could be used to educate parents and their children to the possibility of depression and help them understand the context and ways of helping.

Much needs to be done. The Defeat Depression campaign guide *So Young So Sad So Listen* (Royal College of Psychiatrists, 1995) for parents and teachers is a start, as is the recent publication *Child Health in the Community, a Guide to Good Practice* (HMSO, 1995). *Together We Stand: the Commissioning, Role and Management of Child and Adolescent Mental Health Services* (HMSO, 1995) stresses the importance of educating purchasers of services. In the United Kingdom, many purchasers assume that purchasing mental health services for children entails buying child psychiatry and similar services. The latter report highlights, for the first time, that everybody from school teachers to general practitioners need to be involved if we are really to help children and adolescents with depressive illness.

As purchasing decisions are now being driven by evidence-based health care research, it is possible that, as the outcomes of treatments for all kinds of mental health problems, including depression are difficult to evaluate, this will be used as a justification for not supporting these services fully. This will be a great mistake. From the earliest age, children deserve a service that ensures recognition and appropriate services for all forms of mental disorder. Brave purchasers have major decisions to make if they are to have any impact at the level where it is most needed. If they do not then the future is uncertain.

We have moved forward a long way since Holt (1898) first described the deaths of marasmic infants in hospital, since Freud and Burlingham (1943) first described the profound affective and developmental changes amongst babies who were transferred to nursery care in the Second World War, and Spitz and Wolf (1946) first described what they termed anaclitic depression in infants. The work of Bowlby (1980) and Fraiburg's work amongst very poor families in Chicago (Fraiburg, 1980), creating stimulating intervention techniques to alter the status quo, have all been milestones along the way. Those at the cutting edge of such advances have learned to listen to parents and to believe them (Trout, 1988). Parents have tried so long to tell us about their infants' and children's capacities – stories that we have all too often in the past dismissed.

For these reasons we must be cautious in recommending treatments and panaceas such as day care for all, or supporting a new fashion in parent education that is short on evidence of effectiveness. We must also be cautious in uncritically accepting recommendations for the treatment of childhood depression. For instance, we don't even yet know for sure what constitutes appropriate training to work effectively in the area of child mental health. We also don't know how to be sure that current techniques of research are appropriate when working with infants, children and families (Kazdin, 1988; Kazdin, 1989; Rutter, 1991).

General practitioners have frequently been used by parents in the past to provide information about child upbringing, often reflecting the prevailing attitudes of the time. Reading Truby King and even early editions of what seemed to be at the time Spock's indispensable guide to child care shows how attitudes frequently change – thankfully, usually for the better. It is vital that general practitioners, health visitors and others involved in child care in the primary care team keep abreast of this changing educational environment. We now have to learn a new openness to all the data we collect and analyse, and we must remain ever ready to modify and reform our cherished hypotheses and theories, no matter how challenging this can be.

Fraiburg writes of a moment like this, and those involved in the development and application of mental health policies with regard to children and adolescents would do well to reflect on the implications:

> When David Freedman and I set out to visit Toni (a five month old girl blind from birth due to opthalmia neonatorum) we brought with us a number of hypotheses ... in the next 18 months Toni threw out each of our hypotheses one by one like so many boring toys over the rail of a crib. On the first visit she was making pleasant noises in her crib as we talked with her mother. When her mother went over to her and called her name Toni's face broke into a gorgeous smile and she made agreeable responsive noises. I called her

name and waited. There was no smile. Dr Freedman called her name. There
was no smile. Mother called her name and once again evoked a joyful smile
and cooing sounds. Now, since it's written in our books including my own that
it is the visual stimulus of the human face that elicits smiling in the baby at
three months, Toni's smile had just shattered a major theory. (Fraiburg, 1970)

There are as yet no solutions. Only by ongoing, careful and meticulous
observation, and listening carefully to parents and their children will it
be possible to confront and overcome this most intractable and myste-
rious of illnesses. We will need to learn how to place it within its developmental frame (Kazdin, 1995) without necessarily practising 'top
down' therapeutic interventions that use strategies and treatments
found to be effective in adults and applying them to children and
adolescents (Kazdin, 1989). Instead we need to work from the bottom
up, framing the depressive episode to the developmental stage the child
has reached and learning how to apply the concepts of therapeutic
readiness. We need to recognize, for instance, the phases of psychotherapeutic change (Kratochwill and Morris, 1993). Hopefully research will
enable us to integrate a whole range of interventions at a conceptual
level (Kazdin, 1995) at each point in a child's developmental pathway,
so informing, perhaps, ways to make interventions more successful in
adult life.

References

Bowlby J (1980) Attachment and Loss, Vol 3. Loss, Sadness, and Depression.
London: Institute of Psychoanalysis.
Bowlby J (1988) A Secure Base. Parent Child Attachment and Healthy Human
Development. London: Routledge.
Bowman FM, Garralda ME (1993) Psychiatric morbidity among children who are
frequent attenders in general practice. British Journal of General Practice 43:
6–9.
Cooper PJ, Goodyer I (1993) A community study of depression in adolescent girls,
estimates of symptoms and syndrome prevalence. British Journal of Psychiatry
163: 369–74.
Coverley CM, Garralda ME, Bowman F (1995) A primary care intervention for
mothers of psychiatrically disturbed children. British Journal of General Practice
45: 235–7.
Curtis Jenkins G (1976) Developmental and paediatric care of the preschool child.
Journal of the Royal College of General Practitioners 26: 795–802.
Curtis Jenkins G (1979) Identification of children with learning problems in general
practice. Journal of the Royal College General Practitioners 29: 647–51.
Curtis Jenkins G (1982) The first five years of life. British Medical Journal 285:
1175–6.
Curtis Jenkins G (1992) Working with parents and children, care continuity and
child health surveillance. Queen Charlotte's Hospital, London. Annual sympo-
sium on Child Health.
Curtis Jenkins G, Andren S, Collins R (1978) Developmental surveillance in general
practice. British Medical Journal 1: 1537–40.

Curtis Jenkins G, Newton R (1981) The first year of life (chapter three). London: Churchill Livingstone.

Dadds MR, Schwatz S, Sauders MR (1987) Marital disorder and treatment outcome in behavioural treatment of child conduct disorders. Journal of Consulting and Clinical Psychology 55: 396–403.

Epstein R, Rice P, Wallace P (1989) Teenagers' health concerns, implications for primary care professionals. Journal of the Royal College of General Practitioners 39: 247–9.

Estrada AV, Pinsof WM (1995) The effectiveness of family therapies for selected behavioural disorders of childhood. Journal of Marital and Family Therapy 21(4): 403–40.

Fraiberg S (1970) The Muse in the Kitchen. Smith College Studies in Social Work XL: 2.

Fraiburg S (Ed) (1980) Clinical Studies in Infant Mental Health. The First Year of Life. London: Tavistock.

Freud A, Burlingham D (1943) War and Children? Medical War Books: New York.

Hazell P et al. (1995) Efficacy of tricylic drugs in treating child and adolescent depression, a meta analysis. British Medical Journal 310: 897–900.

HMSO Publications (1993) Seen but Not Heard. London: HMSO.

HMSO Publications (1995) Child Health in the Community, A Guide to Good Practice (part 12). London: HMSO.

HMSO Publications (1995) Together We Stand, the Commissioning Role and Management of Child and Adolescent Mental Health Services. London: HMSO.

Holt E (1898) The Diseases of Infancy and Childhood. New York: Appleton.

Jacobson L, Wilkinson C, Owen P (1994) Is the potential of teenage consultations being missed? A study of consultation times. Primary Care Family Practice: 196–9.

Kazdin AE (1988) Childhood Depression. In Marsh EJ, Barkley R (Eds) Treatment of Childhood Disorders. London: Guilford.

Kazdin AE (1989) Identifying depression in children, a comparison of alternative selection criteria. Journal of Abnormal Child Psychology 17: 437–57.

Kazdin AE (1995) Bridging child adolescent and adult psychotherapy directions for research. Psychotherapy Research 5(3): 258–77.

Kendall PC (1994) Treating anxiety disorders in children: results of a randomised clinical trial. Journal of Consulting and Clinical Psychology 62: 100–10.

Kratochwill TR, Morris RI (Eds) (1993) Handbook of Psychotherapy with Children and Adolescents. Needham Heights MA: Allyn & Bacon.

Mutale TIR (1994) Attitudes of general practitioners and child psychiatrists to treatment methods. Psychiatric Bulletin 18: 668–9.

Royal College of Psychiatrists Publications (1995) So Young, So Sad, So Listen. A Guide for Parents and Teachers. London: Royal College of Psychiatrists.

Rutter M (October 1991) Services for children with emotional disorders. Needs, accomplishments and future developments. Young Minds Newsletter 9: 1–5.

Spitz R, Wolf K (1946) Anaclitic depression. An inquiry into the genesis of psychiatric conditions in early childhood. Psychoanalytic Study of The Child 31: 461–91.

Smith R (1992) Crisis in teenage health. British Medical Journal 304: 1001.

Todd RD, Geller B (1995) What is the prevalence of depression in young people? Current Opinion in Psychiatry 8: 210–13.

Trout M (1988) Infant mental health. Monitoring our movement into the twenty-first century. Infant Mental Health Journal 9(3): 191–200.

Tylee A (1994) Personal Communication.

Westman A, unpublished data quoted by Bernard P, Gerralda ME (1995) in Child and
    adolescent mental health practice in primary care. Current Opinion in Psychiatry
    8: 206–9.
Williams R (1992) The need to manage the market. In Shelly P (Ed) With Health in
    Mind, Mental Health Care for Children and Young People. Proceedings of the
    Conference on Action for Sick Children. London.
Williams R (1993) Psychiatric morbidity in children and adolescents: a suitable cause
    for concern. British Journal General Practice 43: 3–4.

Chapter 9
The Way Forward: Developing a Comprehensive Service

PHILIP BARKER

The idea that children and adults can be depressed in similar ways is relatively new, dating from little earlier than the 1970s (Rutter, Izard and Read, 1986). Even in 1972, the fourth edition of Leo Kanner's classic text on child psychiatry made hardly any mention of childhood depression despite containing whole chapters on such subjects as anxiety attacks, separation anxiety, hypochondriasis, obsessions and compulsions (Kanner, 1972). The subject appears neither in the list of contents nor in the index of Kanner's book, although the 'anaclitic depression' that Spitz (1946) described in deprived, institutionalized infants is mentioned. There is a brief (five-page) chapter on suicide in which the following sentence appears:

> Full-fledged mental illness in the form of schizophrenic or depressive psychoses is responsible for children's suicides only in a very small minority of cases. (Kanner, 1972)

This is virtually the only acknowledgement that the concept of depression in children received in a standard text on child psychiatry of the day. The 1970s, however, was a time of rapid advance in child psychiatry and the first edition of the author's own textbook (Barker, 1971) had brief descriptions of both 'neurotic depression' and 'psychotic depression'. There were some ten other allusions to depression in various parts of the book.

After a slow start, the concept of childhood depression has come to be quite widely accepted during the last two decades but much remains to be learned about the nature of the illness and the depressed moods of children. It will not be possible to plan rational and comprehensive services for depressed children until we have more information, particularly in the areas of incidence, prevalence and diagnosis.

Incidence and prevalence

There is reason to believe that the prevalence of childhood depression may be increasing. Ryan and his colleagues (1992) found evidence of a secular increase in childhood onset of affective disorder. Although their study needs to be replicated and was confined to subjects studied at two centres (in New York and at the University of Pittsburgh, Pennsylvania), it suggested that there was a significant increase of these disorders over the course of a single generation – something which has also been found in studies of adult subjects (Joyce *et al.*, 1990; Robins *et al.*, 1984). The increased suicide rates in children reported by Shaffer and Fisher (1981) support these findings. If these increases are real, as they may well be, their causes and associations certainly merit investigation. It seems clear that such increases cannot be attributed to genetic factors because the changes have occurred in the course of a single generation. Genetic influences operate over longer timeframes. We must therefore presume that they result from factors in children's environments. Although we may speculate about what these factors are, hard data are largely unavailable in this area. Such data are, however, starting to become available.

Although research is needed into many aspects of childhood depression, a first priority must be to establish diagnostic criteria. Further research will be of limited value without good diagnostic tools and at least some generally agreed criteria concerning what exactly constitutes 'depression' in children. As previous chapters in this book have shown, some progress has been made in this area although much remains to be done.

Diagnostic issues

The operational criteria for defining affective disorders that were set out in the Diagnostic and Statistical Manual, Fourth Edition (DSM-IV) (American Psychiatric Association, 1995) and the clinical descriptions in the Tenth Edition of the International Classification of Diseases (ICD-10) (World Health Organization, 1992) – both of which seem to have been developed primarily for use with adults – require much use of subjective judgement and are themselves imprecise. Phrases like 'depressed mood most of the day, nearly every day' leave much to the judgement of the clinician. How depressed must the mood be? How much of the day is 'most'? How often is 'nearly every day'? And what about 'markedly diminished interest or pleasure in all, or almost all, activities most of the day, nearly every day'? With criteria as subjective as these, much will depend on the beliefs of those working in the field.

If the diagnostic task is problematic with adults, it gives rise to even worse difficulties when we deal with children. There are fewer established criteria for the clinical diagnosis of depression in children than there are for adults. Neither DSM-IV nor ICD-10 provides specific criteria for use in childhood, as distinct from the criteria for use with adults. Indeed, the section in ICD-10 entitled 'behavioural and emotional disorders with onset usually occurring in childhood and adolescence' contains no category for depression of any sort, suggesting, presumably, that the onset of this condition does not usually occur in childhood.

We are left, then, to use criteria developed for use with adults. Yet, as we all know, children are not just little adults and it does not always make sense to act as if they are. The problem has been somewhat alleviated by the development of certain measuring instruments such as the Schedule for Affective Disorders and Schizophrenia for School-Age Children – Epidemiologic Version (K-SADS-E) (Orvaschel *et al.,* 1982) and the Child Depression Inventory (Kovacs, 1980, 1983), a self-report scale which is perhaps more useful in following the progress of depressive disorders and for monitoring response to treatment than in diagnosis.

We seem now to be in a situation in which the existence of depression in children is accepted by most of those working in the field, but many questions remain. Not only are there no entirely satisfactory diagnostic criteria, but there is also no consensus as to the frequency and causation of these conditions, even though they seem to be increasingly common. We also have limited knowledge about how they should be treated and how they may be prevented.

When we consider adolescents, as opposed to children, the situation is a little different. It has for longer been accepted that, once puberty has arrived, 'adult-type' depressive disorders are possible. Indeed, the older the age group being considered, the greater is the proportion of clinicians who will consider a depressive disorder as being a likely possibility. We have much to learn, however, even in the adolescent age range.

The fact that this book is being written – and it is not the first book on depression in children – is one indication that the professional community is seriously addressing the task of developing services for children with depression. In doing this, however, we need to know just what we are dealing with, how widely accepted the proposition is that children may suffer from these disorders, and what the incidence and prevalence of these conditions are. We also need to know, or set about learning, how to treat and how to prevent these conditions.

Current challenges

Let us now consider the challenges that the depressive disorders of children present to clinicians, researchers, and other professionals, and the reasons why they have proven so difficult to meet.

1. *The need for good diagnostic tools.* As we have seen, the operational criteria in DSM-IV, and the clinical descriptions of ICD-10, require much use of subjective judgement. Having been developed primarily for use with adult patients, and by clinicians working mainly with adults, their applicability to younger age groups needs to be established. Modifications to the criteria may well prove necessary. Although tools such as the K-SADS-E are available, they are not widely used and there is certainly room for better, easily administered, diagnostic methods for routine clinical use.

2. *Children's labile moods.* Children's moods are generally more labile than those of adults. As a group children are also probably more sensitive to their environments. They cry easily and — under most circumstances — they cheer up easily. To most children, happiness also comes easily — at least most of the time. As I write this, my 6-year-old son, who has just returned from a birthday party, is playing with a Batman toy he has just acquired. It appears to be giving him joy to a degree that a person not familiar with children's behaviours and ways of responding to their environment might consider excessive, even abnormal. To me, it seems well within the bounds of normality. But professionals working with children, who are inevitably aware of how labile children's moods can be, and how easily they change, may not be as concerned as perhaps they should when a child appears unhappy. How unhappy a child must be, and for how long, and how often, in order for this situation to be considered a depressive illness remains uncertain.

3. *Language considerations.* Children are generally less able to describe their emotional states and experiences than adults because their language skills are not yet fully developed. In diagnosing depression the clinician usually depends very much on the patient's description of his or her subjective state. Children, however, often lack the vocabulary and the language skills needed to provide us with a clear description of their subjective experiences. The younger they are, the more likely this is to be the case. We must therefore depend, to a larger extent than is the case with older patients, on collateral information, the validity of which may be limited.

4. *The developmental perspective.* It is a truism to say that the child is a developing organism but one that the developers of diagnostic criteria do not seem always to take fully into account. The mental health assessment of children is always complicated in that the assessor is dealing with a developing personality. There is no established 'pre-morbid personality' with which to compare the current presentation of a child. We must consider how much a child's sadness is an understandable or appropriate response to environmental stress of one sort or another, and what the contribution of the child's temperamental style may be.

5. *The shorter history.* When assessing a child, the clinician usually has quite a short history to consider. It is likely that the current clinical presentation represents the first, or one of the first, episodes of depression. The longer the history, and the more previous attacks there have been, the surer the clinician can often be about the diagnosis. The response that the subject has shown to any treatment methods used in previous episodes can also be a useful guide to the management of the present episode.

6. *Problems with the assessment of suicide.* The assessment of suicide risk is important both from a diagnostic point of view and in management. It can present a particular difficulty in children, and the younger the child the more difficult it is. Although suicidal ideation or intent are not necessary criteria for the diagnosis of depression, especially in younger children who rather rarely commit suicide, they are among the questions that must be considered. If they are present, they may support the diagnosis. Young children, however, have a rather limited concept of death and its finality, and may talk about killing themselves or 'committing suicide' without fully understanding what either the phrase or the action really implies. Determining whether a child has a real desire to die when the child does not fully understand what death is presents a big challenge to the clinician.

Developing services for depressed children

Given the above considerations, how should we set about developing services for depressed children? I suggest that we need the following:

Research into the prevalence and incidence of depression in children

A comprehensive service can only be based on good data about the clients it needs to serve. We need to know how common depression is among the different age groups in the population that is to be served. A start has been made with the various epidemiological studies that have been carried out, particularly since the ground-breaking Isle of Wight Study (Rutter *et al.*, 1970; Brandenburg *et al.*, 1990; Cohen *et al.*, 1993). We need to know more about which children are most at risk, – how great the risks are for different groups, the types of depression to which they are at risk, and the natural history of the various types of depression in each age group. Fortunately, information about risk factors and the vulnerability of different groups is increasingly becoming available as a result of the work of a relatively few groups of researchers.

More knowledge about causation

A start has been made in understanding the causes of depression in children but, again, more research is needed. We know that genetic predisposition plays a part. Weissman and her colleagues (1987) have shown that the offspring of depressed parents are at increased risk of both depression and anxiety disorders. Hammen *et al.* (1987) and Hammen *et al.* (1990) have also shown that there is an increased incidence of conduct disorders as well as of depression in the offspring of parents with affective disorders. There is also a close relationship between anxiety disorders and depression in children (this applies in adulthood too) (Rende *et al.*, 1995).

Although genetic factors surely play their part, they are a long way from being the whole story. It seems that genetic and environmental factors usually combine to produce the disordered mood states we encounter. This no doubt applies to children as it does to adults but the relative importance of the two types of factor may differ. Children, with their greater dependence on their families, may be more susceptible to adverse family factors than adults. Hard data on this are gradually emerging.

Monck *et al.* (1994a, 1994b) conducted a study of self-reported mood disturbances in a group of late adolescent girls. They drew the names of 529 girls aged fifteen to twenty from the records of eight general medical practices in north and east London. These girls underwent assessment by means of interviews conducted in their homes and by the Great Ormond Street Mood Questionnaire (Mann *et al.*, 1983). Key relatives completed the General Health Questionnaire (Goldberg, 1972), giving data about themselves, and the girls completed the same questionnaire but giving information about their relatives. Data were obtained about social background variables. The authors concluded that about one girl in five was at risk of developing affective disorder. The one-year prevalence for psychiatric disorder was estimated at 18.9%, and that for depression and anxiety disorders at 16.9%.

This study revealed a significant association between mood disorder on the one hand and parental separation/divorce, maternal self-report of depression and parental unemployment on the other. It appeared that maternal distress and the quality of the mother's marriage were independently associated with the presence of depression and anxiety disorders in the girls. There was no significant association with age or with parental socioeconomic status. Associations such as these, in girls who were at the stage of their development at which they would be expected to start becoming independent from their families, inevitably raise questions about whether the associations might prove to be even greater at earlier ages, when there is normally a greater degree of dependency on one's family.

We know that depression tends to cluster in families. Williamson and his colleagues (1995), using case-control methods, examined the life-time prevalence of depression and certain other psychiatric disorders in the first-degree and second-degree relatives of adolescents with major depressive disorder (MDD). These authors found that the lifetime rates of MDD in the first-degree relatives of the adolescents with MDD were significantly higher than in the first-degree relatives of the normal controls. This also applied to suicidal behaviour. There was a signifi-cantly higher lifetime prevalence of 'other' psychiatric disorders in the first-degree relatives of the adolescents with MDD. When the second-degree relatives were considered, a higher lifetime prevalence of 'other' disorders was found in the relatives of the adolescents with MDD, but not a higher prevalence of MDD.

Such studies are important to our understanding of the nature and causation of depression in young people, but they leave many questions unanswered, especially concerning the mechanisms behind these rela-tionships. They point the way to much-needed further research.

Tools for the early diagnosis of disorders in children

Because children's moods fluctuate a lot in the normal course of their lives, we need sensitive diagnostic tools that can help us to distinguish between the substantial mood variations that children regularly experi-ence and the early stages of depressive illnesses. Easily administered screening devices that can be used in schools and other settings are required.

More information about how to treat depression in children

Many options are available to us when we are faced with a depressed child. In addition to pharmacological treatments, a number of non-drug therapies are available. Discussing those that may be used with adult patients, Scott (1995) lists behaviour therapy, cognitive therapy (of which at least eight models have been described), interpersonal therapy (which is distinct from therapy that targets the family system) and brief dynamic therapy. For the treatment of depressed children we should probably add family systems therapy, parental counselling, play therapy, and bringing about environmental changes over and above those required by work with the family system. Any or all of the above may be needed, but a 'shotgun approach', applying several of them, may not be the best use of scarce resources.

We must use the available resources in the most cost effective way. This means that we should always carry out as full an assessment as possible of both child and family, and of the child's situation in school and other settings. This is likely to give us pointers to the development of a rational treatment plan. Selecting the best treatment options, never-theless, represents a major challenge to the clinician. Although there is good evidence that antidepressant drugs have a part to play in the treat-ment of at least some depressed children, the extent of our knowledge of their value in this age group is limited. Far fewer controlled trials of antidepressant drugs have been carried out with children than with adult patients. This is an area in which we have an urgent need for more information, especially as new antidepressants appear with bewildering (to this clinician at least) frequency nowadays. Research is also needed into the efficacy of the other treatment modalities listed above.

More education of teachers and others who work with children and parents

Given that depression is now known to occur, apparently with increas-ing frequency, in children and adolescents, we need to make this infor-mation widely known to all who may be in a position to identify children who may be depressed, and to inform them of the warning signs that may indicate the early stages of the development of depressive conditions.

School teachers are one of the groups most in need of this informa-tion. An early indication of the onset of depression is often a falling off of the child's school work. Other changes in the child's behaviour and relationships with other children may also be observed. Day care workers and others who work with children – for example foster parents and the staff of group homes and other institutions that care for chil-dren – also need this information. Such information should be incorpo-rated into the training of such groups.

Parents also require this information, and those who have themselves suffered from depression, or currently do so, must be made aware that their children are at greater risk than the general population of children. Indeed, closer links between those providing psychiatric services for adults and those dealing with children and adolescents would seem to be very desirable. My own clinical experience is that depression in chil-dren seldom comes to light because clinicians treating depressed parents have taken the trouble to enquire whether any of the children in the family have shown evidence of depression.

An interesting initiative is that of the American Academy of Child and Adolescent Psychiatry (AACAP), which has taken to the Internet to provide information for the public. The AACAP, like so many other orga-nizations, has established a home page on the World Wide Web (<http://www.psych.med.umich.edu/web/aacap/>). It provides a link to a sub-page entitled 'Facts for Families'. At the time of writing, this contains forty-six 'information sheets' designed to inform and educate parents and families about psychiatric disorders affecting children and adolescents. One of these deals with 'The Depressed Child'. Among the subjects addressed by other sheets are 'Children of Parents with Mental Illness', 'Know When to Seek Help for Your Child', 'Questions to ask about Psychiatric Medications for Children and Adolescents' and 'The Anxious Child'. These may be copied without payment, provided their source is acknowledged. There is also a need for the education of family physicians, public health nurses and other health professionals. They all need to become aware both of the real possibility that their child patients may be suffering from depression, and of fact that there is a greater likelihood of this if there is a history of depression in their families. Many health professionals currently in practice received their training before there was general acceptance of the frequency of depression in children, and they may be unaware of some of the relevant recent research in the area. These are subjects that need to be addressed in the continuing education of such groups. The Internet may also be a useful way of keeping mental health professionals informed.

The specific groups of children who are at increased risk of becoming depressed include:

- Those with a family history of major depressive disorder.
- Those who have been sexually abused. Stern *et al.* (1995) compared eighty-four sexually abused children with children randomly selected from alphabetical lists of children matched for age and sex in the general school population. They found that the abused children had more depression, lower self-esteem, and more behaviour disorders.
- Those who have suffered neglect and/or other forms of abuse. Brown and Moran (1994), in a community survey, found that the experience of neglect or physical or sexual abuse in childhood is an important predictor of chronic depressive episodes in adult life. It is more than likely that the pattern of depressive response is set well before adulthood in many cases. Brown *et al.* (1994) found that this also applied when they studied a patient population consisting of female psychiatric patients treated in the psychiatric departments of two London hospitals.

The way ahead

Where does all this leave us? I suggest that three stages are necessary in the development of a comprehensive service for depressed children. The first is the recognition that depression in children is a reality and that the condition is common. This has, on the whole, been achieved. The second is the study of depressed children, including their family, school and wider environmental contexts. This is the stage we are in at present. There are encouraging signs – of which this book is but one – that we are making progress in this.

The third stage, on which we have scarcely embarked, is that of discovering how to prevent the development of depression in young people and how to treat it. Prevention may prove to be the biggest challenge of all but we are beginning to learn who may be most at risk, an important first step. The use of the Internet may prove to be a cost-effective means of disseminating knowledge, which may contribute to prevention, early diagnosis and even, through providing up-to-date information to professionals in the field, more effective treatment.

To achieve comprehensive treatment services we need much more research into both pharmacological and non-pharmacological treatment methods. We need to know which are effective in which clinical situations, how to combine different treatments, and how to use them all in the most cost-effective ways. This will surely take us well into the next millennium, but I am sure it will be a well worthwhile endeavour.

References

American Psychiatric Association (1994) Diagnostic and Statistical Manual of Mental Disorders, 4th Edition. Washington DC: American Psychiatric Association.

Barker P (1971) Basic Child Psychiatry. London: Staples Press.

Brown GW, Harris TO, Hepworth C, Robinson R (1994) Clinical and psychosocial origins of chronic depressive episodes. British Journal of Psychiatry 165: 457–65.

Brown GW, Moran P (1994) Clinical and psychosocial origins of chronic depressive episodes, I: A community survey. British Journal of Psychiatry, 165: 447–56.

Goldberg D (1972) The Detection of Psychiatric Illness by Questionnaire. Maudsley Monograph 21. Oxford: Oxford University Press.

Hammen C, Burge D, Burney E, Adrian C (1990) Longitudinal study of diagnoses of children of women with unipolar and bipolar affective disorder. Archives of General Psychiatry 47: 1112–17.

Hammen C, Gordon G, Burge D, Adrian C, Jaenicke C, Hiroto D (1987) Maternal affective disorder, illness and stress: risk for children's psychopathology. American Journal of Psychiatry 144: 736–41.

Joyce PR, Oakley-Brown MA, Wells JE, Bushnell JA, Hornblow AR (1990) Birth cohort trends in major depression: increasing rates and earlier onset in New Zealand. Journal of Affective Disorders 18: 83–9.

Kanner L (1972) Child Psychiatry. Springfield IL: Charles C Thomas.

Kovacs M (1980) Rating scale to assess depression in school-aged children. Acta Paedopsychiatrica 46: 305–15.

Kovacs M (1983) The Children's Depression Inventory: A Self-Rated Depression Scale for School-aged Children. Pittsburgh: University of Pittsburgh School of Medicine.

Mann A, Wakening A, Wood K, Monck E, Dobbs R, Szmukler G (1983) Screening for abnormal eating attitudes and psychiatric morbidity in an unselected population of 15-year-old schoolgirls. Psychological Medicine 13: 573–80.

Monck E, Graham P, Richman N, Dobbs R (1994a) Adolescent girls: I. Self-reported mood disturbance in a community population. British Journal of Psychiatry 165: 760–69.

Monck E, Graham P, Richman N, Dobbs R (1994b) Adolescent girls: II Background factors in anxiety and depressive states. British Journal of Psychiatry 165: 770–80.

Orvaschel H, Puig-Antich J, Chambers W, Tabrizi MA, Johnson R (1982) Retrospective assessment of child psychopathology with the Kiddie-SADS-E. Journal of the American Academy of Child Psychiatry 21: 392–97.

Rende R, Wickramaratne P, Warner V, Weissman MM (1995) Sibling resemblance for psychiatric disorders in offspring at high and low risk for depression. Journal of Child Psychology and Psychiatry 36: 1353–63.

Robins LN, Helzer JE, Weissman MM, Orvaschel H, Gruenberg E, Burke JD Jr, Regier DA (1984) Lifetime prevalence of specific psychiatric disorders in three sites. Archives of General Psychiatry 41: 949–58.

Rutter M, Izard PR, Read PB (1986) Preface. In Depression in Young People. New York: Guilford.

Ryan ND, Williamson DE, Iyengar S, Orvaschel H, Reich T, Dahl RE, Puig- Antich J (1992) A secular increase in child and adolescent onset affective disorder. Journal of the American Academy of Child and Adolescent Psychiatry 31: 600–5.

Scott J (1995) Psychological treatment for depression. British Journal of Psychiatry, 167: 289–92.

Shaffer D, Fisher P (1981) The epidemiology of suicide in children and young adolescents. Journal of the American Academy of Child Psychiatry 20: 545–65.

Spitz RA (1946) Anaclitic depression. In Fenichel O (Ed) The Psychoanalytic Study of the Child 2: 313–42.

Stern AE, Lynch DL, Oates RK, O'Toole BI, Cooney G (1995) Self esteem, depression, and family functioning in sexually abused children. Journal of Child Psychology and Psychiatry 36: 1077–89.

Weissman MM, Gammon GAD, John K, Markings KR, Warner V, Prusoff BA, Sholomskas D (1987) Children of depressed parents: increased psychopathology and early onset of major depression. Archives of General Psychiatry 44: 847–53.

Williamson DE, Ryan ND, Birmaher B, Dahl RE, Kaufman J, Rao U, Puig-Antich J (1995) A case-control family history study of depression in adolescents. Journal of the American Academy of Child and Adolescent Psychiatry 34: 1596–607.

World Health Organization (1992) The ICD-10 Classification of Mental and Behavioural Disorders: Clinical Descriptions and Diagnostic Guidelines. Geneva: WHO.

Index